What Readers Are Saying about
SALES WISE

What great stories! It's a very enjoyable read and the stories bring out so many of the key points that one needs to be successful in sales.

— *Stephen Crain,* VP *Sales*

I found the book inspiring, informative, an easy read, and insightful ... for anyone attempting a sales job.

— *Craig MacMullen, Small Business Owner*

Sales Wise is a real good yarn ... and each chapter provides a useful message to the reader. It made me question whether or not I had always appeared this way in front of my clients.

— *Barry Gauthier, Sales Executive and Business Entrepreneur*

I was expecting light stories ... what I found was something deeper, more comprehensive, a teaching text. I am probably the textbook example of someone who should read this book—an entrepreneur with no past professional sales experience. This is the sort of book that should be read and reread.

— *Varda Treibach-Heck, Start-up Company Founder and* CEO

Sales Wise

*A Journey Through
Sales and Selling*

Martyn Lewis

Sales Wise: A Journey Through Sales and Selling

Copyright © 2006 Martyn Lewis. All rights reserved. No part of this book may be reproduced or retransmitted in any form or by any means without the written permission of the publisher.

Published by Fenestra Books®
610 East Delano Street, Suite 104
Tucson, Arizona 85705 U.S.A.
www.fenestrabooks.com

International Standard Book Number: 1-58736-442-5
Library of Congress Control Number: 2005934315

Contents

Acknowledgments vii
What's It All About? 1
Prologue 5

A Sales Odyssey

(Complete) Competitive Intelligence 13
Selling Around the Holes 15
Turning Over Rocks 18
Know Your Customer 21
ATQ 26

This Pilgrim's Progress

When Know Means Yes 31
The Corporate Pitch … and Toss 34
The Fear Factor 37
Chickens Don't Always Stay Counted
(or … Never Stop Selling) 39

Getting Better All the Time

Sell from the Inside Out 43
The Elusive Decision Maker 45

Who Is Setting the Pace? 48
The Proposal Team 52
The Cost of Delay.................................... 56
www.com Is Not a Friend of Today's Sales Professional. 58

Fables

For Want of a Jack.................................. 63
The Case of the Floating Volvo 67

Sales World

Show Your Stuff—by Asking Questions? 73
Lights ... Camera ... Action!......................... 76
When a Pencil Is More Than a Pencil................... 82
Do You Know Why Someone Will Buy from You?.......... 86
Companies Fund, People Buy......................... 89
Finding Value Finds Customers....................... 90
Yours Sincerely 93
The Large Account Management Paradox................ 95
Are Objections Objectionable?......................... 99
The Price Is Too High—Oh, Really? 103
So What?.. 106
The Difference between Interest and Commitment 108
What You Know ... and What They Want............... 111

The Final Word

A Look Back....................................... 117
"I Don't Want to Be a Salesman" 123

Acknowledgments

I must admit that I used to skip over the acknowledgments in each new book I picked up. That changed when I started writing myself and realized that there is one huge gap between thinking of writing a book and actually seeing the words on the pages of a published book. I cannot imagine sitting down to accomplish this task without the help of others.

In my own case, I must start by acknowledging Tom Percy. Tom has been a friend and business colleague of mine for many years. His insightful advice has rarely proved wrong. He too has had many years of successful selling experiences. Tom collaborated extensively with me in writing this book, but more than anything, he took my rough drafts and crafted the words that are now on these pages.

I would also like to acknowledge all the sales professionals I have worked with, and especially those who have acted as mentors to me. Of course, some of the more memorable folk and situations I have been involved with are captured here in this book. In most cases I have disguised their names, but who knows, you may just recognize yourself. Thanks for providing such a treasure trove of memories and material.

Finally I would like to acknowledge my mother, Iris. From the beginning she imbued in me the value of persistence, of remaining positive in attitude and thought, and that if you want it badly enough, anyone can really achieve anything. For providing me with these and so many more values, which have proved vital in a career of sales, I dedicate this book to her.

What's It All About?

I am a sales professional. I wasn't always one, and I certainly didn't start my career thinking that this was where I would be now, but here I am. And it seems only natural that when you find your true calling, you seek to identify that exact place or moment when you realized that this is it, this is what I do, this is what it's all about. Here's how it happened to me.

Many years ago I happened to live next door to a rather fine TV journalist. When I turned on the TV at 6 or 11, I would see what my neighbor had been up to all day. One evening over the backyard barbecue, we were chatting about what we both did for a living. I knew nothing about journalism and so was intrigued to discover how she spent her time.

Seemingly, journalists have to discover new stories, search for leads, and then conduct research. They have to knock on doors and talk to people who don't necessarily want to talk to them. They need to have great questioning and listening skills. They need to act quickly and respond to deadlines. They have to collect and absorb great volumes of information, and then present that in a succinct and meaningful manner.

Sound familiar? I was somewhat amazed at the similarity between our roles. It seemed as if journalism and sales had a lot in common. I shared with her some of my day-to-day activities and she was also somewhat surprised at the similarity between our roles. In any case, she remarked as such and we both mused on that for a while. Then, with the sort of epiphany that can happen on a summer night over drinks and dinner, I realized that there was a vast chasm of difference between her job and mine.

Journalists investigate and report on events, but they stand metaphorically to one side—detached, reporting, but not involved.

Sales professionals also engage in these activities, but then take the giant leap, cross the line, *and get involved*, and for only one reason—to make a difference.

Sales professionals seek to change the course of events to the mutual benefit of the company they represent and the customer to whom they are selling. They change a customer from buying from a competitor to buying from their company. They change a customer from buying next month to buying this month. They change a customer from buying the standard offering to buying the top-of-the-line product. Sales professionals make things happen. And when you think about it, if salespeople did not actually change the course of events, there wouldn't be much use for them.

In my years as a sales manager I have unfortunately met far too many salespeople who would make better journalists. They report to their company about what their customers are doing or what the competition is doing. They report to their customers about what their own companies are doing. They report to their peers about who they saw and what they heard. They've got spreadsheets and presentations and white papers and articles and a lot of reporting is happening, but few if any events are changing.

As sales professionals, we must exhibit many of the practices and skills of journalists. We must carefully research our opportunities, nurture our contacts, develop leads, and investigate situations. We must have excellent questioning and presentation skills, but we must never lose sight of the fact that

What's It All About?

all of this activity is being undertaken for one simple reason: to change the course of events.

In your own selling endeavors, are you a reporter or a sales professional? Are you observing, or are you changing the course of events?

Prologue

Sales is a great profession. My days (and years) in sales have offered me some of the most challenging and indeed rewarding situations in my career. I have learned many lessons. Some of these have been about how to sell more effectively, others include how to improve my business skills, while still others have had valuable life lessons associated with them. And it's mostly been a lot of fun. Conversely, my sales days also include some of the most frustrating times that I have ever known, and no more so than that first couple of quarters that I was on quota.

I was educated in England and started my career armed with a degree in computing and a vision of becoming some sort of crack programmer. This was in the pre-Microsoft/BlackBerry/broadband era when computers were the size of houses, radiated the heat of a small blast furnace, and boasted price tags that could rival an emerging nation's GDP. But there I was, where I wanted to be and doing what I wanted to do, and my career progressed through a number of technical positions and eventually evolved into the position of project manager.

In this role, it was my job to support a sales team selling mainframe computers costing several million pounds (and weighing not much less), and so for the first time in my career, my work brought me into direct contact with salespeople on a daily basis. I became involved in understanding client requirements, designing solutions, writing proposals, and making presentations. And on completion of a successful sale, it was my responsibility to lead my team to install, test, and hand over a working system to the now technologically advanced though somewhat fiscally diminished client.

Now, at that time I have to admit that salespeople were something of a mystery to me. They certainly wore expensive suits, drove cool cars, lived in large houses, and played a lot of golf, and who could have a problem with that? But as far as I could tell, their talents seemed to be limited to the gift of gab, the ability to wine, dine, and entertain prospects, and in the little time they spent in the office, corralling a team of people to do the *real* work with their prospects and customers. And the really strange thing was that the company I was working for kept trying to move me into sales. It was my belief—and indeed I said so to my boss—that, "Why would I want to be in sales? I have a degree!"

Well, time passed and when I moved to North America it seemed to me that in order to advance my career into the ranks of more senior management, I should actually get some real-life sales experience on my CV. I looked upon this as a sabbatical of sorts—take a year or two off from the real world of bits and bytes and go play with the customers. I had worked with many salespeople, some good and some bad. I certainly knew the cut of a good suit, enjoyed driving fast cars, and accredited myself well when handed the wine list, though my golf needed a lot of work. Well, three out of four's not bad, and besides—I actually knew what I was talking about. So I reckoned that I would really ace this job.

What a shock I received.

I had no idea what salespeople had to do to make their quotas and even less of an idea about all the extraneous and time-consuming stuff that lands in a sales rep's lap. It became very apparent that there were many questions that I had no answers for—and these were tough questions that needed answering right away. For instance:

Prologue

Where do prospects come from?

Delivered by a stork? Lined up outside my office? I hadn't really given this much thought. I guess I had always imagined that there was a continuous supply of prospects eagerly waiting to talk to our sales folk. Of course what I knew for sure was that the technology solutions that our company offered were vastly superior to the competition's and that they delivered unquestionable value to our customers.

How do you get someone interested?

Once again, I somehow must have thought that people were benevolent in providing their time to salespeople, and that these people were actually looking forward to the visits of sales reps to enlighten them. Especially considering our vastly superior technology solutions that delivered unquestionable value.

How do you get someone to actually part with money in exchange for your offering?

I had worked on some great business cases while supporting sales teams and I knew my way around a business justification and return on investment (ROI) presentation as well as anyone. I thought that there could be little doubt that prospects would be eager to invest in our offerings when there was such a rich payback, considering our vastly superior ... etc., etc.

I obviously hadn't given much thought to these questions, or many others as well. To me, the selling process was a series of fairly straightforward steps.

First, meet with prospects.

Prospects that identified themselves to you—or at the very least, when they were contacted, would be happy to meet with you.

Second, tell them all about your products and services.

I wasn't totally naïve here; I did realize that I should do my homework, find out about their company and industry, and then put together some sort of customized presentation so that the benefit of our offering became apparent and relevant to them.

Third, put together a proposal, together with a good business justification, for presentation to the prospect.

Finally, handle any last-minute questions they may have, and of course secure the order, pick up the check, and ring the big bell.

It swiftly became obvious—and I mean as obvious as a tree falling on your house, and with similar results—that this approach was not going to cut it. I not only lacked the fundamental skills of the sales game, but was also painfully unaware of the hundreds of little details and real-world situations that are part of the day-to-day existence of a professional salesperson.

For instance, I had no idea that when my company advertised a new product to be ready for delivery in ninety days, it could often take three or four times as long to actually materialize on the customer's shipping dock. And I especially had no idea that I'd often be the last one to find this out, and the first one in the company that my customer would beat on. I was also unaware that the competition's offerings were very good, and in some cases even superior to our own. I just had no idea, and the list goes on and on.

However, toward the end of my initial six months on quota and with some battle experience under my belt, things started to get clearer to me. I was also very fortunate in having had a number of great mentors—people who to this day remain among the best sales and businesspeople I know. Many of these people were good enough to share their experiences and practices with me. And so my knowledge of the profession and the processes of sales grew and it still grows.

Prologue

After almost twenty-five years in sales, having managed thousands of salespeople and worked with many thousands more, I am still learning.

I have also learned that there are many salespeople who are as inadequately prepared for selling as I was back in the early eighties. Some carry the title of sales, but many others do not. I have come across many small-business owners and entrepreneurs whose very livelihood depends upon their ability to persuade someone to buy into their vision, their company, and therefore their offerings. Many of these folks do not consider themselves salespeople, but just like I did, are learning the hard way about what it takes to discover and close a prospect.

It is through working with all these various people that I have been encouraged to share a number of my favorite selling stories. With the exception of a couple of fables, each one is true and each one I hope carries a valuable learning lesson. Even a veteran sales pro may look at things a new way through some of these stories or, like myself, may just enjoy remembering their own favorite selling moments or conversely relive their worst nightmares, albeit nicely soothed by the balm of time.

Throughout *Sales Wise*, I look at the mountains and dragons and oceans that have confronted me, and at how my efforts to climb them, slay them, and cross them have shaped and developed my outlook and insights into the business that is sales. At the end of each story, you will find a powerful and, I hope, helpful learning experience, and I'll summarize these again at the end of the book.

So read and enjoy, and even if you don't recognize yourself in some of the stories, I hope you recognize some of the situations and learn how one salesperson coped with them. Maybe it will help you on your long and winding road, sales-wise, anyway.

A Sales Odyssey
The Early Years

(Complete) Competitive Intelligence

In the early eighties I moved from the UK to Canada, and in so doing I left one large computer vendor and joined another. As a newbie sales representative I was obviously anxious to learn the ropes and start selling, and as with any new sales hire I was also subjected to much sales training in my first few months. Most of this training was not actually sales training—it was product training. We had to learn the feeds and speeds and bits and bytes of an impressive array of different hardware and also the relative merits of a wide selection of software.

Within the curriculum was what initially appeared to be extensive knowledge about our competition, and much information was provided to us on how our products and offerings stacked up against theirs. There were many "us vs. them" charts, which almost invariably showed that the "us" offerings were superior—often vastly superior—to the "them" products.

"Well," thought I, "it would seem that this overwhelming product advantage should translate into absolute market dominance and surely the easy attainment of all sales quotas. I'd better go out and buy a large suitcase to carry all that cash to the bank." That was when a little red light started blinking in the back of my mind and, as I'm sure you've guessed, this was not quite the case—and herein lies the issue.

A Sales Odyssey

Having just arrived from one of the competitors, I actually knew the "them" column for that company better than the "us" column. The very latest and even in some cases yet-to-be-announced technology from my new company was being compared to my former company's products of three to five years before. And compounding the issue was that the manner in which the information was presented clearly favored the "us" products.

Of course I later found out that this was not just an isolated case in this particular company. Overly enthusiastic engineers and marketing people often provide this type of information to the sales force, and I'm reasonably sure that in the majority of cases they do not intentionally seek to lie or misrepresent the truth in any way. They just love their own products, and their enthusiasm can often lead to overemphasizing the attractiveness and uniqueness of their offerings while downplaying the competition. And to give them the benefit of the doubt, it can indeed be difficult to get complete and up-to-date competitive intelligence.

Although your company's competitive intelligence can be useful, never rely on it alone. All too often the information provided can be out of date or incomplete, and there is no substitute for doing your own legwork. Third-party reports and independent analysts can be valuable sources of competitive intelligence and comparisons. See if you can actually get your hands on the latest products from your competitors, or ask users of competing products what they like and don't like about these offerings.

To be successful in selling, you must understand your competitors' offerings and how yours stack up against them. However, gain that competitive intelligence in as many independent ways as possible—especially from current customers. There is nothing quite as powerful as hearing from actual users how they rank your offerings against the competition.

Selling Around the Holes

I will never forget my first national corporate sales meeting. We were a large company so I was there along with several thousand other sales folk—and I was pumped. Freshly pressed suit, shiny new briefcase, and my imagination bubbling over with that unbridled, fearless optimism that you cannot believe anybody else in the room can come close to. Of course I have since learned that many felt exactly the same way and indeed still do, and thank goodness they do. Sadly, these large gatherings are fast becoming a thing of the past, and it's too bad in a way because there was something very special about the buzz of a large national sales convention. Surrounded by your peers, revved up with competitive anticipation, and all like-minded in enthusiasm—and especially if it's out of town.

So there I was, and as is typical the first day ended with a dinner for the multitudes followed by the keynote address from our corporate vice president of sales. In more recent years, I too have been that after-dinner speaker and I've discovered it can be a tough role to fill. What does make it easier is when you realize that if you're the VP of sales, just about everybody in the room eventually reports up to you. Then, as now, the audience was clearly attentive.

To add to the excitement, the leader of our sales force was an almost legendary character with a booming voice that hardly needed the help of a microphone. As is typical on these occasions, he shared with us his rationale for his unshakable belief in our future success. After presenting us with all the reasons he believed we would continue to be market leaders, imagine my surprise when he changed gears and said,

"We know that in some cases our products have a few holes.

"We know that our competitors' offerings are not that far behind us.

"We know that at times our customers see certain weaknesses in our overall offerings.

"We know that at times our competitors leapfrog us in some areas."

Wow! I couldn't believe that a senior executive of the company would actually admit that we didn't always have the best mousetrap. And it was what he said next that has stayed with me all these years.

"And we don't need *you* to tell us—we pay other people to tell us this. *Your job is to sell around the holes*. If we always had the best products and our prospects and clients always viewed us as the best solution provider, we wouldn't need a sales force. The only reason that we have you is to sell around the holes."

Interesting words indeed, and a point well worth making because since then I have unfortunately met too many salespeople spending too much of their time dwelling on why they can't sell. They make it a significant part of their day, sharing with anyone who'll listen what the competition is doing better than *us* and why *we* could be in trouble. I've seen too many sales meetings turn into major whine sessions as soon as the manager leaves or when the floor is thrown open for discussion. So in my mind, there is a real lesson to be learned from the words in that after-dinner speech.

Now, not for one moment would I suggest, nor do I believe, that our VP of sales was suggesting that we lie, cheat, or steal our way to fame and fortune—but we have to

Selling Around the Holes

realize that our competitors are no slouches. And hopefully we have ample confidence in our own company, our own offerings, and our own ability to provide a successful solution to our customers. Perhaps in a perfect world we could pick our spots where our offerings and only our offerings were the ideal solution for the customer, but reality suggests that you're not going to get to quota-heaven with that plan. So it becomes abundantly clear that a very important part of our job is to guide the sales situation around the holes that may exist in our offerings and play to the strengths of what we can provide to our customers. Because that VP was probably right; if we always had the perfect product, why indeed would we need salespeople?

Don't waste your time complaining about the competition and other factors you can't control; focus on the strengths of your own offering and what you can control.

Turning Over Rocks

During that rookie year I had a sales manager who insisted that we spend one day a week doing outside cold-calling. As I was selling computer systems, the concept of selling such large-ticket items door-to-door seemed somewhat suspect to me and I was very doubtful that it would lead to any productive results. I tried to convince him that I had better and more effective ways to spend my time, but he was the boss and so out I went. At the end of the week we had to provide a report covering who we had called on and what the outcome was.

For the first few weeks, I really did not look forward to Wednesday's door-knocking. So I tried another tack and tried to convince my manager that it was just as effective and more efficient if I stayed in the office and made telephone calls. He still wasn't buying, so back out I went. Interestingly enough, after weeks of kicking against this concept and a few weeks of actually doing it, I realized how much I was learning by getting out there and talking to people face-to-face. Even if I didn't get past the receptionist, I would learn all sorts of things about the company by their facilities, their reception area, and other indicators that you could only notice by being there.

I also learned to sniff out territories where others had not been recently. That's how I discovered Cornwall—a small city on the Saint Lawrence River that had its fair share of industry but was a couple of hours drive from both Ottawa and Montreal and had therefore escaped the scrutiny of the majority of other computer sales folk. So each Wednesday I would get up slightly earlier and head off to the paper mills and light industry of Cornwall. Each week I would pick one location in the morning and one in the afternoon, park the car, and start walking from door to door in the industry estates.

Late one morning I stopped by a manufacturer of fiberglass bath/shower stalls. I asked at the reception area if there was someone I could talk to about computer systems. She asked me to wait a moment and then a large, older, and somewhat gruff character came around the corner to talk to me. He asked me where I was from and what I wanted. Well, it turns out that he was the retiring owner of the business, having just sold the company to a larger conglomerate. Even more interestingly, he actually had one of our systems running his operation. More interesting still, it was this very computer system that stood between him and his much-desired retirement.

He explained to me—as if it were my fault—that the computer system had to communicate over the phone line to the new owners of the business and was failing to do so, despite several days of effort. I asked to see what he had and he took me out back and introduced me to the individual who was trying to get this piece of equipment working. Well, it so happened that I could immediately tell that they had the wrong multiplexer board and could swap that for the correct one for about $2,200. I even gave them the name of one of our distributors where they could get one the next day.

Not surprisingly, his attitude toward me changed very quickly, as I turned from foe to friend. He asked me if he could buy me lunch and off we went to a great local fish restaurant. Over fish and chips, he asked me what the heck I was doing in this remote industrial area. I explained that I was discovering what businesses there were and what they

A Sales Odyssey

were doing for their computer systems. Well, he said, his daughter just happened to be the executive assistant to the local manager of one of Canada's largest research companies, and would I be interested in meeting with him? You bet! One phone call later, I was confirmed to meet with him at 4:00 P.M. that day.

It turns out that he was about to sign an order in excess of $1 million for two computer systems from one of our competitors and didn't really realize that there were alternative approaches. Six weeks later—thanks to cold-calling and turning over rocks—I had my first million-dollar order.

As sales professionals, we must make an effort to turn over every rock in our path. Take the time to network, discover who's who and what opportunities there may be lying under those rocks.

Know Your Customer

I had often heard it said that the easiest person in the world to sell to is another salesperson. Now, I wasn't quite sure where this idea came from; perhaps there was an unspoken bond between salespeople such that when presented with a good pitch they rewarded it with their business. Or maybe salespeople were so used to truly believing everything they said about their own products that they assumed that other salespeople were a bastion of truth and integrity as well. Either way, it seemed yet another fascinating mystery to unlock in this brave new world that I had entered. And are sales folk the easiest people to sell to? Well, after what happened in the following story, I came to the conclusion that I guess it depends on who that salesperson is.

After a couple of years of successful selling, I decided to forgo my company car and buy a car of my own. Now, I'd long had my eyes on a BMW, and one evening I happened to be in the vicinity of the local dealership—purely by coincidence, I can assure you—and decided to drop in to see what was new. There it was—a brand new, dark blue 318i with all the goodies. Now, yes, it was the entry-level model, but that didn't matter; this was my car, my BMW. I started chatting with the sales rep and after some polite haggling we settled on a mutually agreeable price, I duly paid a refundable deposit, and I headed home. The deal would be complete when I showed up the next day to sign all the paperwork and drive away in my new BMW—YESSS!

A Sales Odyssey

The next morning I could hardly wait to tell Mike, a peer and fellow sales rep who worked in the cubicle right next to me. Now, Mike happened to be a young single guy who I think it would be fair to say was quite ambitious and was no slouch when it came to image consciousness. He favored Hugo Boss and Armani suits with the appropriate Italian shoes to match, and just generally breathed a greater air than the rest of us when it came to style and fashion. Mike also drove a company car and had also been talking about buying a BMW for quite some time. Talk about the ultimate one-upmanship opportunity—if I were only that shallow.

When I shared the good news with Mike that I had bought a BMW, his comeback was to tell me that he had actually given up on the idea of a BMW and had moved on to the vastly superior Audi. He related to me all the great features that the Audi had over the BMW, with a not so subtle implication that I was something of a fool to buy a BMW and not an Audi—indeed, he was only days away from buying one. And I have to say that he managed to rain more than a little on my parade.

After further discussion we agreed that we would check out both of them over the lunch hour. We would visit Audi first—after all, I could still back out of my deal on the BMW with no penalty. If we were not sufficiently impressed with the Audi, we would then go on to the BMW dealership where I would firm up my order and Mike would take a look at the latest models that they had to offer. The clock seemed to move a little slower that morning, but finally it was noon and we were off.

We arrived at the Audi dealership and started looking around. Eventually, and I do mean eventually, a salesperson materialized to unlock the model on the showroom floor. We checked it out, with Mike highlighting all the great features that the Audi had over the BMW—all the time underscoring the folly of my purchase decision. We asked the salesperson if we could take a test drive. Somewhat grudgingly he agreed, but insisted that he would need our driving licenses and we'd have to fill out various forms before being allowed on the road in one of their demonstrators. The paperwork duly completed, we headed out into the lot.

Our not-so-friendly salesperson found the car (which was dirty) and as he was maneuvering it out of a rather tight parking spot, we couldn't believe it when the Audi logo fell off the front grill. We pointed this out to him and he got out of the car and popped the logo into his pocket with the explanation (as if it was a benefit) that the cars were often vandalized because people in that neighborhood liked Audi logos, and—get this—the dealership left them loosely attached so that when they were stolen there would not be too much residual damage to the car. This had either happened before or the guy was really fast on his feet. Either alternative was not encouraging.

Anyway, he got back in the car and pulled up to where we were waiting, and he decided to turn on the windshield washers to at least clean up the forward visibility. I guess the washer jets had never been adjusted and they promptly started spraying windshield washer fluid on the front of Mike's suit. As Mike jumped back in horror, the salesperson leaned out the window and said, "Well, if you can't afford the cleaning bill, you can't afford this car." And then to top things off, the guy drove us once around the block without even offering to let us drive, and as we were pulling back into the lot he fired off his parting shot by saying, "I bet you boys can't wait for the day you can afford one of these puppies."

We left somewhat speechless. To give Mike credit, though really ticked about the suit, he was undeterred and made some comments about another Audi dealership across town that would now get his business. Needless to say, my mind was made up.

We arrived at the BMW dealership and there was my new baby in all its gleaming glory. I was shown to a desk in the showroom where I started going through the paperwork, and as I was signing the necessary documentation that would let me drive the car away, Mike ambled around the showroom.

After a few moments my own salesperson introduced me to the sales manager. He thanked me for my business and after pleasantries I returned to completing the paperwork. The sales manager then struck up a conversation with Mike. He asked him if he was interested in BMWs or thinking of a car purchase. Mike gladly informed him that he was looking at the Audi. I was nothing short of totally shocked when I heard the sales manager agree with Mike that the Audi was a great car. Not only that, he shared with Mike that they probably lost more customers to Audi than any other manufacturer. He went further—he suggested that Mike might have been impressed with the extra interior space, the larger trunk, and the extended warranty. Mike of course was in full agreement, and my only explanation for this strange turn of events was that maybe the sales manager was about to quit BMW and join the Audi sales team.

I could tell Mike was enjoying this apparent put-down of the BMW, and right in front of me as I was completing the paperwork for my new car! But then a funny thing happened; the sales manager went on to say, "Just look around you on the road—who's driving Audis? It's the family man, the guy who now has a wife and kids and needs that extra room and all that trunk space. We lose more business from the older family guys to Audi than I care to mention. Contrast that with who you see driving BMWs—the younger, successful, career-minded professional. I just wish there were more of them."

Know Your Customer

We left the dealership somewhat later than planned—both in our new BMWs.

I don't know if it really matters what car you drive, but as a salesperson I surely know that it really matters that you know who your customer is.

Always know who your customer is and what they need to satisfy their own dreams, wants, desires, and goals.

ATQ

Back in those dark ages before laptops, notebooks, Palm Pilots, BlackBerries, cell phones—indeed all of the wonderful time-saving, labor-reducing, user-friendly, leading-edge devices that we just cannot function without—we used to carry around briefcases. Hardly a sales rep in those days did not have one, often a hard-sided Samsonite, and the style and look of these had a fair bit to do with the internal one-upmanship within the sales team. There was the standard smooth finish black model, some opted for the brown pebble-grained look, and the odd brave soul even went for the faux alligator in deep burgundy.

Along with these various potential fashion/ego statements, one feature that just about all of them had was a little space under the handle where you could stick those embossed self-adhesive initials. This feature also spawned a little hierarchal horseplay in the team pecking order. Some of the rookies would have those initials right up there front and center, while a few of the veterans coolly ignored them as being just a little tacky.

Another mitigating factor, of course, was the *deadly initial acronym* syndrome. You'd never see initials on briefcases belonging to Albert Steven Sanders, Sandra Alice Porter, Fred ... well, I'm sure you get the picture. And then there were always those few sensible folk who just thought it was a good idea, for identification purposes if nothing else—bygone reminders, perhaps, from the days of Mom putting nametags on their school clothes.

ATQ

So one day, I was out on a sales call with one of our reps and noticed the letters ATQ on his briefcase. Not too much wrong or outstanding about that until you know that his name was Ray and his initials were RJT. One thing you should know about Ray is that he definitely marched to a different drummer, so I assumed that perhaps he had borrowed (stolen? inherited?) the case from an Andrew T. Quinn or some such person, or maybe he had a little inside joke on the go—I didn't know. However, one thing I did know was that Ray was also an exceptional sales professional—one of the best I've ever known.

A little while later I had a chance to ask him about the briefcase and those initials, ATQ. He laughed and explained that he'd purposely put those initials on his case. Why? Because ATQ stands for one of the most powerful selling tactics I know and it was there to always remind him to **A**sk **T**he **Q**uestion. As he reached for his briefcase at the end of every meeting, he would always see the initials and be reminded to Ask The Question.

The question may be asked in a number of ways, but it invariably starts with the same four words ... "Is there anybody else ..."

Is there anybody else I should be talking to?

Is there anybody else who may be interested in talking with me?

Is there anybody else who will be involved in this decision?

Is there anybody else you know that you could refer me to?

What do we find out from these questions? Well, all of us who have been involved in cold-calling or prospecting know the value of a warm, friendly body. A referral is, hands down, the most effective way to start any new selling relationship. If someone who has already given you their time (and, even better, their business) will now give you a name of one of their contacts—it is gold. To then follow up and call on this new name and confidently state that Jennifer Client or Joe Customer gave you their name as someone that they considered would be interested in talking to you—this is worth a hundred cold calls!

Another great reason for asking the question: If you are into a selling situation and you ask if there is anyone else you should be talking to, you may hear something you don't want to hear or weren't expecting. But it will save you a lot of time and grief by finding out sooner rather than later. You may hear ...

"Oh, you should be talking to Jim; he has the budget for this."

"I guess we should go talk to Mary in purchasing; she has to authorize all these purchases."

"Nilesh, my boss, will have to be involved."

These, and responses like them, can reveal who should be contacted, whose advice and cooperation you will need, who will help, and who will hinder a successful close.

Two solid reasons to Ask The Question: you'll find out more about what you need to know in that particular selling situation, and you'll discover all about the easiest and loveliest sale of them all—the referral.

2 This Pilgrim's Progress

When Know Means Yes

One of the nice things about working with great sales professionals is that I've also been associated with some very significant competitive wins. There are, of course, many factors involved that contribute to a big sales win, and one immediately thinks of such things as price advantage, superior product quality, great timing, and some plain old good luck. But when I think of all the factors that these situations have in common, there is one overwhelming characteristic. Let me share with you this story of a true sales professional.

Steve was a young salesperson on my team many years ago. He had all the attributes that most of the other members of that team had: enthusiasm, extensive product knowledge, and a keen desire to succeed. But what set Steve apart were two important characteristics—a doggedness that would not quit, and a commitment to roll up his sleeves and get involved in the hard work. These are qualities that don't always readily show themselves, but they came into play when he uncovered an opportunity that could lead to a contract in excess of $40 million the following year. The operative word here is "could," and this opportunity was a long way out, meaning that it would not contribute to his (or my) current quota. And there were two major hurdles to overcome: our competitors had a long and significant relationship with the key players in the prospect's organization, and they likely also had a superior product offering. Not an appealing situation for most salespeople, and few would fault those who would pass on it and get on with other things. But to Steve, the allure of the big win combined with his tenacity and commitment motivated him to take on the challenge—thankfully.

When I later analyzed everything, it became clear that Steve had first set himself two major objectives: to find out as much as possible about the prospect and as much about the competition as he could. He set about learning everything he could find about his prospect's business. He would talk to anyone and everyone who would let him in the door. He sought to find out not only what they were planning, but also why they were approaching things the way they were. He spent countless hours researching their organization, their corporate history, and the industry they were in; not an insignificant task in those pre-Internet days. He volunteered to take on all sorts of tasks just to better understand what their operation was all about, and he probably spent more time on their premises than on our own.

At the same time, he managed to not only learn everything he could about the incumbent supplier who would be the main competition, but also who most likely the other competitors would be. He actually contacted other companies that were customers of these competitors to see if he could glean any information about their strengths and weaknesses. He was becoming almost obsessed with the situation and, quite frankly, as his sales manager I was starting to worry, as Steve was doing little else these days.

But there was no stopping him, and it paid off when we got into the proposal process and he could really show his stuff. When it came time to write our proposal, Steve arguably knew the prospect's requirements better than they did. And herein is the common factor across these big wins—*the top salesperson totally understands the needs of the prospect*. When they received our proposal, their people could easily see the depth of understanding that Steve had of their needs, their priorities, their fears, and their desires. It was obvious to them that he (and by association us) really cared about their organization, knew it inside out, and was vitally interested in their success. We won that business; we weren't the cheapest, and arguably other companies may have had better products, but we had a vastly superior knowledge of what they wanted.

The knowledge and understanding you have of your prospects will be clearly apparent to them when you demonstrate how well your solution meets their needs. This is of an inestimable value because it can illuminate concerns and issues that may otherwise be left unwritten, unspoken, and therefore unaddressed; and it's all due to your superior knowledge of the prospect. When interacting with sales professionals who clearly understand their needs, the prospects will trust those individuals and have a far greater tendency to select them over the competition.

It is too often that salespeople try to differentiate their offerings strictly on price or features and benefits. The real winners differentiate themselves by their in-depth knowledge of the prospect's situation, and can turn "know" into yes.

The Corporate Pitch ... and Toss

I was involved a few years ago in a very important strategic selling situation. A large IBM customer was considering a new technology platform, and the opportunity of unwinding a Big Blue system (intoxicating to the say the least) beckoned. IBM clearly had the inside track and our work was certainly cut out for us. Now, as it happened, I had a pretty good contact within the organization. Jim was a senior executive, part of the evaluation team, and was a close friend of a close friend. We moved in the same social circles, often dined together, and had visited with our wives to each other's homes. Jim had often let it be known that the current system needed replacing, and so over time he had become "the guy I knew" there. We all like to have one of those, don't we? I was thinking that Jim would be a valuable resource.

After several months of intense selling efforts—evaluations, presentations, proposals, and all the other various and sundry activities that give salespeople gray hair, ulcers, and great golf swings—we were short-listed with two other suppliers including the incumbent IBM. The customer then told us that they would dedicate a full day to meeting with each of us and that a decision would follow shortly.

Finally, exactly what I was looking for: face-to-face, one-on-one, and us with our corporate guns locked and loaded with valuable and relevant information. I had comprehensive profiles of each of the executive team members who would be attending the presentations. From some of Jim's earlier

The Corporate Pitch ... and Toss

comments I felt I was able to understand what they were looking for and what was important to them, and what they did and didn't like about the other two finalists. The contract was worth several million dollars, would clinch our quota for the quarter, and included the added major bonus—a badge of honor for knocking off IBM, and in those days that was a very bright and shiny decoration indeed! It could very well be our day in the sun, and we set to work.

Well, you can imagine the time and effort we put into preparing the presentation. We flew in industry gurus, application specialists, and technology experts from across North America. We designed a multimedia extravaganza in our state-of-the-art customer presentation center that was worthy of a Broadway production. We even ran a full dress rehearsal the day before the big show. Along with the optics and the sizzle, we also had substance on our side. We knew what the customer was thinking. We knew what the customer wanted. We could not have been better prepared.

The big day arrived and it went off flawlessly. We shared our understanding of their business challenges, discussed and demonstrated how our technology would provide them with a competitive advantage, and discreetly advised of where we believed we were better than the competition. When we were done, there were warm handshakes all round and they thanked us sincerely for a very productive day. The evening ended with me buying dinner for the team that believed they had done a great job—and they had!

It so happened that I had arranged cocktails with Jim the next evening. We met and of course I was much anticipating his feedback. It was really no surprise when he shared with me that his team had really enjoyed the day and believed that it was time well spent. He said that everyone fully realized the expertise we had brought to the occasion and how they agreed that our solutions would enable them to gain competitive advantages in their marketplace. At this stage I was positively glowing and I truly believed that there was only a rubber stamp standing between us and the contract. And then the roof fell in.

What he said next absolutely floored me and has stayed with me for all of my selling years. Jim said, "But you know, there really is very little difference between what you said and what the other two suppliers said. In fact, you are almost indistinguishable." After my initial shock, he shared with me that there were far more similarities among the three finalists than differences—right down to the suits we wore and the decor in our meeting rooms.

IBM kept the business—when presented with little difference, why change?

From this I learned a very valuable lesson—assume that your competition is just like you. Don't think that you can differentiate yourself based solely upon your own products and services. Assume that your competition understands the market and that they know the right words to say. Assume that their teams are as equally dedicated and professional as yours.

Don't get hooked into thinking that your prospect is going to sit through your corporate sales pitch and unquestioningly believe that you are better than your competitors. Your prospect will probably be just as excited or just as bored with your pitch as they were with everyone else's.

The Fear Factor

When involved in a selling situation, many sales professionals become fearful of discovering information that may slow down or derail an anticipated win. As soon as they're engaged with a prospect that shows a real level of interest, they want to get a proposal in front of them and go for the close. Why ask what the budget is, only to hear that there is no budget assigned as yet? Why ask about time frames, only to hear that they are not going to be ready to make a commitment until next year? Such responses stop progress—they prevent the deal from closing, they mean lost commissions, missed forecasts, and undoubtedly some red faces at the next business review meeting. As a friend of mine once said, the last thing on their minds is setting up their own hurdles. So it's press on regardless, hoping that this will be the one where the stars actually do line up, hell freezes over, and the prospect will sign the contract as soon as we put it in front of them. This reluctance to discover information that just may be bad news I call the fear factor.

I recall a big opportunity that was being managed by Andrew, an experienced senior sales rep, accompanied by Jennifer, a new rep, who was tagging along to learn the ropes. A proposal had been issued and the team was planning the closing call. The strategy that was emerging was simple: make the call that Friday, go through the proposal, and ask for the business. However, throughout the planning meeting, our eager, inexperienced sales rep Jennifer was constantly asking questions about the competition. The seasoned account manager, who had not heard the prospect mention anything about competitive bids, repeatedly brushed off her comments. To her credit, Jennifer hung in there and insisted that we should find out if there were any competitors in the picture. In frustration, Andrew finally exclaimed that it would slow things down and complicate the strategy if they asked about any alternatives that they might be considering, and might even cause the prospect to think about going to the competition. His tenure won the day and the team went off on Friday to close the business.

Imagine the embarrassment when rather than sign the deal, the prospect said that they had been working with a competitor for the previous four months. And further, they were just checking with us to see if our approach was any different from or significantly cheaper than the competitor's service they were already using. It became abundantly clear that we were simply being used as a counterbalance to keep the incumbent provider honest.

Maybe if Jennifer with her youthful enthusiasm had been managing the opportunity, the real situation would have been discovered earlier, resulting in a very different selling strategy and probably saving a lot of wasted time and effort.

I find that the fear factor tends to intensify the closer a deal gets to the order. If the salesperson thinks that the customer is very close to making a commitment, the last thing they want to hear is anything that may prevent that from happening.

Don't get caught by the fear factor. Even if you fear what you may hear, ask questions to discover what the situation really is before investing time and effort in the wrong opportunities.

Chickens Don't Always Stay Counted (or ... Never Stop Selling)

Mike Lee was competing for a major contract at a large manufacturing company. The Request for Proposal had been received, examined, and completed. Much activity had transpired between his team and Susan Hanson's, the chairperson for the prospect's purchasing committee, and Mike knew he was on a short list of two finalists. Over the next few weeks his team worked hard on several presentations and discussions, all of which led to some tough but mutually beneficial negotiations. Just after lunch on a Friday before a long holiday weekend, he received the phone call that we all live for.

"Hi Mike, Susan here. Just wanted you to know the good news before the long weekend; we have decided to go with you guys. Let's get together next week and go through the details."

Well, needless to say there were high-fives all around the office. Celebrations lasted well into the evening and the team left for a well-earned long weekend. The following Tuesday, and in great anticipation, Mike patiently waited for Susan's call and wasn't overly concerned when he hadn't heard from her by end of day. The guess was that she was busy catching up as he himself had been doing all day. However, his patience wore thin by Wednesday lunchtime and Mike figured he'd better call Susan himself to start scheduling the meetings to put the contract in place. He tracked her down and two minutes later his world imploded when he learned that Susan had already finalized and signed a contract with the competition. Are you kidding me?

Here's what happened. Right after she'd called Mike on Friday, Susan decided that it would only be fair to call the other short-listed potential supplier prior to the weekend as well. No high-fives for sure, but the never-say-die sales rep from the competition asked if there was any way that Susan could possibly spare twenty minutes on the holiday Monday. Due to some good positioning and a sense of fairness, she agreed to meet him Monday morning. Needless to say, *that* team did not enjoy the long weekend; they worked around the clock at crafting a more imaginative proposal and further honed their approach to see how they could better meet Susan's organization's requirements. They did such a great job and demonstrated such commitment that they won the deal, *and* they also made sure that the successful closing meeting was not considered over until they had a signed contract in hand. And to throw a little more salt in the wound, they were actually more expensive than Mike's proposal.

There is an old selling adage that you never celebrate a deal until the order is signed. In the car business, they say the deal isn't done until you see tail-lights over the curb.

Never stop selling until the order is signed, because chickens don't always stay counted.

Getting Better All the Time
Sell from the Inside Out

Sell from the Inside Out

"They must understand that we can ..."
"They should see that we ..."
"We should tell them that ..."
"Don't they realize that ..."

The "they" and the "them" in these quotes refer of course to prospects, and I always shudder when I hear such statements. The epitome for me of such dubious reasoning was what I heard once from the CEO of a start-up organization. Full of the confidence and, in this case, the myopia that sometimes come from an unassailable belief in one's own products, he was blathering on to his salespeople that the prospect "should consider it an honor to do business with us. Tell them that our product is the best on the market. Tell them that major companies are doing business with us. Tell them that we have worked on this technology for over five years and hold several patents." Would they care? Some perhaps might, but most probably wouldn't.

This is a clear example of an often abused though time-honored style of selling: bombarding the prospect with information. We'll regale them with all the things that we consider wonderful and unique about our products, hoping to raise their enthusiasm to the same fever pitch of our own. We almost want to say, "Stop me when you hear something you like." We then expect the prospects to do our work for us, hoping that they will be able to sort through the data and quickly extract that which rings their bells and pushes their buttons.

Getting Better All the Time

Now, it is not surprising that many employees tend to have a somewhat overvalued opinion about their own company's products and services, and this is not necessarily a bad thing. It's obviously commendable to have a strong level of loyalty to and belief in your company. However, there's an intrinsically dangerous element in having such an undying faith in your own product, and this is often joined with underestimating the competition. We are then faced with the only logical course of sales action—attempting to educate the prospects to such an extent that they will develop the same level of enthusiasm and the same blind faith in our offerings that we have ourselves. Ultimately this rarely works and can often backfire into a massive waste of time and resources.

Rather than practice this soapbox selling style of overwhelming our prospects with information, what we really need to do is better understand what our prospects are all about. Dr. Steven Covey, in his book *The 7 Habits of Highly Effective People*, describes this with his usual clarity when he declares, "*Seek first to understand, then to be understood.*"

I call this selling from the inside out. Start with listening, not telling. Discover what matters to the prospect. Define what it is they value. Find out more about who these individuals are. What are their past experiences? What are their preferences, priorities, needs, wants, desires, fears, and anxieties? Based on this understanding, we can then position the value of our service and solutions to their own unique needs.

Pull information out of a prospect rather than push information in—sell from the inside out.

The Elusive Decision Maker

Many sales methodologies and selling tactics still focus on locating and selling to the decision maker. We've all heard it—sell high, go to the source. And indeed, why not? If you can find that one person in the organization who can say "yes," why bother wasting time with anyone else? Just find out what they want, present a compelling offer, and close the business. If only life were that simple!

This style of selling is firmly rooted in the 1980s and before. For those of us who remember the eighties, you may recall that you could hardly open a business magazine or attend a business keynote address without hearing about networked organizations, empowered employees, and self-directed work teams. This whole movement evangelized the philosophy of softening corporate autocracy in favor of moving the decision-making ability down in the organization and breaking down vertical silos in favor of cross-functional teams. Did you ever wonder what happened to all those articles and speeches? We're living them—it has actually become the way we work today. And while many organizations may not fully embrace all aspects of the movement, most of today's companies are far more networked, utilize many more cross-functional processes and teams, and indeed have pushed significant parts of the decision-making process across and down in the organization.

In today's corporations there is rarely a single decision maker, but rather a series of mini-decision makers involved in most purchase cycles. There may well be a needs-analysis team, a procurement group, along with a competitive analysis process in place—all of which provide advice in a team format when major purchases are being considered. While the final funding may need to be approved by a single person, perhaps the CEO, that person is rarely the lone decision maker. In most cases, that person would be the caretaker of the overall process but not the single decision maker in the traditional sense of the word.

Now, one would think that along with this evolution of the purchasing process, a parallel evolution of the selling process must have occurred. Well, actually no, because if it had I'd most likely be in a different line of work and you wouldn't be reading this book. Putting it nicely, there are many indications that the selling process has not kept pace with the purchasing process. And whom we spend our time selling to is one of those indications.

When we are selling to today's organizations we must make the commitment and take the time to fully understand this network of decision makers. We need to know who is likely to be involved in the evaluation and investment process. It's a fool's game to try to shortcut this process, and attempts to do so will usually backfire and cause delays in the sales cycle. It is not difficult to imagine what goes through a CEO's mind when presented with a proposal for perhaps a new software application or new shop-floor equipment. He or she is very likely to say such things as, "Is John in manufacturing onside with this? What did Mary in production say? How about Larry in HR, and Pat in finance?" If any of these people who have a vested interest in the purchase have not been involved and have not been advised and helped with their part of the decision, your sales efforts are guaranteed to be stalled at best, and at worst probably finished.

The Elusive Decision Maker

When selling today, lose the notion of the mythical single decision maker—odds are there isn't one. Get to know and understand the total network of all those who influence the purchasing decision.

Who Is Setting the Pace?

As part of my consulting work, I have the pleasure of sitting in on many sales meetings, coaching sales teams, and doing what I can in sharing best practices. It's probably one of the most enjoyable parts of my job as I get to work hands-on with selling teams in their day-to-day world. Typically these meetings will include reviews of specific sales opportunities. A sales professional will brief his or her manager about the opportunity and, after being updated, the sales manager will often then follow the briefing with an enthusiastic and productive barrage of questions—to the salesperson, an interrogation. After many aspects of the situation are exposed, discussed, and resolved, they hopefully will agree upon a decisive plan of action designed to move the sale forward. Here is part of a session that I sat in on fairly recently.

After the comprehensive grilling, John (the anxious new sales guy) says, "So, that's about the situation at Long Wharf Manufacturing."

To which Susan (the enthusiastic sales manager) concludes, "Well, John, from what you have told me, there really isn't a budget to fund our proposal."

"Well, not at the moment."

"But did they like our proposal?"

"They didn't like the first one, so we changed it."

"Oh?" says Susan.

"And we nearly got it with the second."

"Yes?"

Who Is Setting the Pace?

And now John warms to the discussion. "But we really nailed it with the third proposal I presented to them last month. They love the configuration, the price is right, and it really seems to work for them."

"That's great, John—so where's the money going to come from and when will they buy?"

"Well, they think they may get the budget next month, but it's still a little up in the air."

"So, John, what do you think the next step should be?"

"Well, Mark Johnson—he's the CFO and the guy who makes the money decisions—told me they have a budget meeting on the eighteenth of next month, so I've marked in my calendar to call him on the nineteenth and see if the funds received the green light—fingers crossed."

"Okay, sounds good. Thanks, John, and keep me posted."

Perhaps a typical review conversation, but I think there is an opportunity here. How about talking to Mark Johnson today as opposed to the nineteenth, and asking what it would take to get the funds approved as opposed to when they are going to be approved? Even if we get a negative response we may be able to discover why, and perhaps even find out what is getting funded. The point that I would like to highlight with this situation is the difference between customer-driven and sales-driven sales cycles.

Every sales/buy cycle comprises a number of trigger events—events that must happen in order to move the situation forward. A funding approval is a great example of such a trigger event. Others may include:

- » getting the okay from other individuals within the company;

- » completing an internal assessment;

- » deciding to go with one alternative approach over another;

- » completing another project upon which this was dependent;

- » approving a business case.

These all represent important and decisive trigger events, and here's a funny thing about them: As earlier defined, they not only move the sale forward but perversely could hold up the sales cycle as well. If they are under our own control, it is obvious that we should take action on them as quickly as possible. But if they are under the control of our prospect, then we should not sit and wait. Otherwise we end up with a customer-driven sales cycle in which we are always waiting for the customer to take action. They are setting the pace and they are driving the deal.

As salespeople we should be doing whatever we can do to set the pace. We should not only be asking when the budget might be approved, but what it would take to get such approval as early as possible. We should be investigating to see what we can do to drive the sales cycle at a faster pace than it would normally move—i.e., at our pace. We should find out who we have to get in front of, what information we should be getting, what other departments might be involved. Is an RFP going to be issued? If so, who's defining the requirements and decision criteria? We should be continually striving to set the pace so that we are driving the deal.

You will not always be successful with these inquiries, but I can guarantee that you will discover interesting and potentially useful information. Maybe if John in the above example discovers that the funding will only be green-lighted when they can show how the investment ties into another strategic

Who Is Setting the Pace?

initiative in the company, he will have the right information to put together a fourth—and winning—proposal.

We should shift from asking when something will happen, to finding out why and how we can make it happen. Set the pace, rather than react to the pace that is being set by the prospect.

The Proposal Team

We were recently working with a company that was tight on resources, many people doing double duty and all being sensitive to efficient results. Not surprisingly, they were interested in how they could become even more effective and efficient—essentially achieve more results with equal or less effort. We took a detailed look at their processes and activities and found something very interesting. Among the more than fifty people in their sales organization, three people did nothing except prepare and respond to Requests for Proposals (RFPs) that the company received.

Now, most of us know that RFPs are found across all industries but are very prevalent in large bureaucratic organizations and especially government institutions. The reasons are simple—these organizations have to give all possible vendors a fair shot at their business and can't be seen to be favoring one company over another. And especially in the case of public-sector purchasing, the belief is that open RFPs ensure that the purchasing organization will get the best bang for its buck and therefore be a prudent and fiscally responsible minder of the public purse. To further understand the process, let's follow the life cycle of the procurement process in such an organization. Each phase could last anywhere from a few months right up to a year or more.

The Proposal Team

Phase 1:
- » Identify a need and examine various ways with which to proceed.
- » Apply for a budget for the next fiscal period or beyond.
- » Wait.

Phase 2:
- » Get provisional budget approval.
- » Meet with a number of potential suppliers to investigate the market.
- » Formulate what is required.

Phase 3:
- » Take the requirements and specifications and issue an RFP to a number of potential suppliers.
- » Wait.
- » Evaluate the response to the RFP.
- » Select the best supplier from the responses.
- » Negotiate and contract.

Now, I realize that what I've described might sound somewhat simplistic, but quite frankly it is not that far off the mark. And what we must really keep an eye on is what happens between Phase 2, *Meet with a number of potential suppliers to investigate the market,* and Phase 3, *Take the requirements and specifications and issue an RFP to a number of potential suppliers.* Because herein often lies the brutal truth.

If we are selling a complex product or service—as opposed to a strictly commodity-type offering—there will always be a number of unique aspects to what we have to sell. It may be the only one available in blue, or that will tolerate temperatures in excess of 150 degrees, or that comes with

Getting Better All the Time

two operating languages as standard. And like it or not, the suppliers—especially the smart ones—who meet with the prospect prior to the RFP being issued often have the opportunity and certainly have the motive to *shape* that RFP. The smart sales professionals will be in there with their advisor hats on, being a source of information and expertise and therefore a resource to the prospect. Before you know it, the RFP is asking for the color blue, the ability to withstand a temperature of 150 degrees, and two operating languages as standard. This means that unless you were in and talking to the prospect and helping to define their requirements, the likelihood of winning such an RFP contest is remote indeed.

So let's get back to the company I introduced you to at the start. With the VP of sales, VP of marketing, and the CEO all in the room, I asked them how many of these open RFPs they had bid on and how many they had won, keeping in mind that their proposal team was in place solely to respond to RFPs where there had been no previous contact with the prospect. They calculated that they were likely bidding on three to four of these a month and had been doing so for nearly two years, but not one of them could really recall any that they had won. The CEO actually rushed out of the room to get the RFP log, and when he returned he had a look of horror on his face. They had won only three—and in each case, the RFP team had actually written the proposal as a favor for one of the salespeople who had been in talking to their prospects (and no doubt helping shape the RFP). In other words, their dedicated proposal team had an actual track record of zero over two years of responding to open RFPs—not a very good return on investment for a company priding itself on running a fiscally tight ship.

Many companies and sales professionals can't resist the temptation to respond to RFPs. But the facts are very clear, in most situations—you have

The Proposal Team

less than a 5-percent chance of winning if you have not been working with the prospect prior to them issuing the Request for Proposal. Either make sure you are in early helping the prospects define their needs, or don't waste time and resources in bidding on open RFPs.

The Cost of Delay

Several years ago I was CEO of a company with a growing staff, and we were looking for expanded office space in Toronto. The economic climate at the time was decidedly recessionary and it was a good time to be looking—it was definitely a buyer's market. I teamed up with Ken, my chief financial officer, to investigate various locations of downtown office space. He was there to provide his usual prudent and pragmatic fiscal advice—and also, I suppose, in case I perhaps got carried away with breathtaking views or close but irrelevant proximities to enticing extracurricular entities.

We were shown a very suitable location in one of the new high-rise complexes and we were walking around the site with the landlord. It had everything we were looking for, and knowing glances passed between Ken and me. So we offered so much a square foot and what we believed to be a fair price, but after the usual sighs and calculator manipulations our offer was declined. However, we both knew that we weren't that far from a deal. And then out of the blue, just before we were leaving, Ken used a great tactic that reminded me of an effective old selling tool concerning the cost of delay. He glanced upward and started counting the ceiling tiles, which incidentally were approximately one square foot in size. This went on for a moment or two and then he turned to the landlord and said, "Do you know that each one of those ceiling tiles is costing you about $14 a month just to keep up there?" And we left.

The Cost of Delay

The cost of delay. In this case it meant that for every month that the site stood empty, it was costing the property management $14 for every one of those tiles, and I can assure you that there were a lot of tiles. We could only assume that after we left, the property owner looked up himself and got back on his calculator, because later that day they took our offer and we signed the contract.

This was a cost of delay. However, the tactic can easily be used the other way around. If you are, as I hope, truly providing value to your prospects, you should be able to quantify the cost of delay. What would it cost them in hard cash every month by putting off buying from you?

How much could they be saving?
How much revenue would they be losing?
How many clients are lost to a competitor?
How much market share are they losing?
How many people are leaving their organization?
How is their competition advancing?

All through your sales cycle and especially prior to negotiation, know and quantify what the cost of delay is for your prospect.

www.com Is Not a Friend of Today's Sales Professional

The proliferation of corporate Web sites, a virtually mandatory exercise in today's business environment, is a phenomenon that is obviously here to stay. I find it strange that companies are investing significant amounts of money in their Web sites and doing so because they largely believe it to be a great selling tool. Unfortunately, those of us involved with generating new customers know otherwise. Today, too many prospecting calls are met with, "Give me your URL, and we'll call you back if there's anything we're interested in." In my darker moments, I sometimes wish that the people who get so excited about putting all this great information online were the ones who had to actually go out there and get a new customer. Not that I want to be labeled as being anti-Web; obviously in many ways it is a great marketing tool. But it is no friend of the salesperson trying to get in to see a new prospect.

When I was selling computer systems in the early eighties, I used to be able to get in to see prospects as they had little choice if they wanted to learn about my company and its products. We were the information highway of all that was new, and in many cases the customer even looked forward to seeing the sales reps if only to keep up on the latest and greatest. We held little regard for the salespeople who, in response to a prospect's request for information, would just send off a brochure. One of the most ineffective selling lines had to be, "I'll send you our information kit, and will call you later." Invariably there was little or no response to such a phone call, or at best a "Thank you for the information; we will let you know."

This brings to mind a great expression I learned a long time ago—*the selling stops when the brochure is delivered.* And whenever I say this I usually hear gasps, especially from marketing people. But isn't it true? When we deliver all that great information to a prospect, haven't we just given up on the primary selling role? We have essentially dumped all the information on the prospect with an implied "Hey, you work it out." We are asking our prospect to take a look through all our material and see if there is any interest in what we have. Professional selling? Not!

So how does all this relate to the Web? Well, when you think about it, the Web site is not only delivering the brochure (and more), it is doing so at warp speed. And as there is little or no interaction between the prospect and the salesperson, we rarely get to know who is actually interested and even less about what they're interested in. What corporate Web sites have done is fundamentally change and potentially delete a key role of the sales professional—the salesperson is no longer the primary conduit of information between the vendor and the customer.

So what can we do? Well, actually, it's more like what shouldn't we do. For starters, the last thing we should be doing is using the Web like the old sales information kit. Do not tell prospects to go to the Web and see if there is anything of interest. Despite the great efficiencies of the Web, we must use it in a positive fashion. Use it as you would use any good piece of marketing collateral; pick your spots, make it part of a great presentation, and show only what is relevant to that specific situation. The effective sales professional must still meet with prospects to understand their needs, desires, preferences, anxieties, etc.

Of course, if there is no value in this interaction with a prospect, then by all means send everyone to the Web and disinvest in the sales force. In this case you are truly commoditized and the salesperson is just an expensive information messenger. However, in the vast majority of selling situations, the sales professional should be able to add value to both the purchase and the sales process. Remember, if the selling stops when the brochure is delivered, then the selling also stops when you simply provide your Web site address.

See the Web for what it is: an electronic sales brochure. Don't invite your prospects to wade through all the information on the Web—get in the door and discover who they are and what they want.

For Want of a Jack

It was a dark and stormy night. A young man, Nigel, we'll call him, was driving down a remote country road in the small hours of the morning. He vaguely knew the area—mostly small farms—and he'd read about the occasional out-of-office politician, a retired author or two, and a few other gentlemen farmers who chose the secluded lifestyle of the country. But it was dark and wet and Nigel had other things to worry about.

As is sometimes the case, at the worst time and in the worst place, one of the car's tires blew out. Despite the dark remoteness of the place and the lateness of the hour, there was little option but to get out and change the tire. So out he got and started fishing about in what is to most of us that mysterious area under the trunk floor where rumor has it a spare tire lurks. Unfortunately—with Murphy smiling down on him—the tool kit hadn't been checked recently and the jack was missing. The spare tire was there and so was the lug-wrench, but no jack. So there was little left for Nigel to do but lock the car and start walking in search of help.

After walking along the road for quite a while, he finally saw what looked like a farm in the distance and started walking purposely toward it. As he got closer, he saw that it was indeed a farm and he began mentally rehearsing what he was going to say if the farmer opened the door—at one o'clock in the morning. "Sorry to bother you, but I've had a blowout and wouldn't you know it, there doesn't seem to be a jack in the car—you don't happen to have one that I can borrow?" Well, in the middle of the night, that seemed not only a little inadequate but also proof positive that the farmer was looking squarely into the face of incompetence personified.

Nigel got closer and started agonizing over the fact that the farmer would of course be asleep and he was going to have to wake him up—"Does that mean I'll have to pound on the door?—I don't want to pound on the door," he thought. And then he came to the worrying conclusion that no one in their right mind was going to react very favorably to being woken up in the middle of the night. And especially a farmer—they get precious little sleep as it is! The poor guy probably had to get up and milk the cows and feed the chickens at the crack of dawn—oh, this was not good. And why would anyone loan an idiot stranger a jack—especially a farmer? He would need it for his livelihood, and he'd be appalled at Nigel's mechanical ineptitude and disgusted with his total lack of responsibility.

Nigel was getting close now and his anxiety level was reaching Richter-scale proportions. He thought about turning back, or searching for an alternative. But there was clearly nobody else and no other help available. With each step, the anxiety and stress mounted until he found himself trembling at the door of the farmhouse.

He knocked timidly on the door. Nothing. He knocked louder, thinking, "Oh, no, I'm pounding." An upstairs window lit up. At this point, Nigel was nanoseconds from just running away, but he hesitated when he heard footsteps walking down the stairs and sensed a shadowy figure approach the door. "He's going to be so ticked off," thought Nigel, his heart pounding. The door opened, releasing a flood of warmth and light, but before the owner could say a word, Nigel blurted out, "Keep your lousy jack, I can manage just fine without

For Want of a Jack

it!!!" He turned and hurried away, leaving a rather surprised and sleepy retired author standing on the doorstep.

The moral of the story is that we so often get all worked up about a situation that we respond more to our own stress rather than the situation itself. I have seen this happen in a number of selling situations. I have seen far too many otherwise capable sales reps who became so convinced that no one would want to take their cold calls that they couldn't pick up the phone.

Here's a real-world example. Sue worked for a very successful company—so successful, in fact, that demand was outstripping supply. Current delivery times had been pushed out to over three months and Sue had convinced herself that this was an insurmountable issue for most of her prospects. I actually sat in on sales calls where she would lead with the fact that because the prospect would probably want a fast delivery schedule and how her company couldn't deliver for three months, there was really little point in exploring any opportunities further. And not unlike the retired author in the farmhouse, the somewhat stunned prospects would sit there and listen to this. They were just trying to get some basic information and the salesperson was actually throwing up problems.

Another instance of this anxiety-producing situation often surfaces in the classic demo. Take the case of Harry, who was selling software for a company that was just slightly behind the latest trends and standards. Their software, quite frankly, was every bit as good as their major competitors' but Harry had convinced himself that they had a big problem due to the lack of their, let's say, JE4 compliancy. Harry's demos would start with him saying, "Now, I have to tell you that we are not JE4 compliant and that could be a problem for you." To which the prospect would probably be thinking, "What's JE4?" The demo would continue and he would say

Fables

such things as "Ignore this screen," and the prospect would ask why and, you guessed it, Harry would say, "Well, it shows that we're not JE4 compliant." Harry was so wound up with his own misperceptions of product failings that he just didn't sound convincing talking about what was really good about his product.

I call these "imagined objections," and they are objections that often only exist in the mind of the salesperson. The salesperson creates them, internally enhances them, and fears them, and this fear can cripple the whole sales effort. And most tellingly, it is usually the salesperson—and often that person alone—who brings these fears and objections to the surface.

Although it is always a good practice to think through what problems may lie ahead, don't react to situations that have happened only in your mind.

The Case of the Floating Volvo

A longtime Volvo owner (whom we'll call Dave) had kept his current model for almost ten years and decided it was time to replace his car. Now, Dave hadn't looked at new cars for quite a long time and as such was not really aware of what was new and exciting in the automotive world. So off he went to his local Volvo dealer and, as is the case in many car dealerships, the sales reps were all busy talking with other customers, prospects, suspects, tire-kickers, the receptionist, and so on. So Dave wandered around on his own looking at all the new models.

Needless to say, he was surprised at the wide variety of models now available—his last purchase had really only involved the choice of sedan or wagon and in what color—and now he saw big sedans, sleek two-door coupes, an SUV, an all-wheel-drive station wagon, and even a pretty convertible. Dave was mightily impressed, but what really caught his eye was what appeared to be a floating Volvo right in the middle of the showroom. And not only did it seem to be floating, but the car had no wheels or tires. Well, Dave was very curious and took a closer look. He looked all over, put his arm under the car, over the car, looked carefully for any wires, magnets, or whatever else might be holding the car up. Nothing.

Just at that moment, a sales rep (whom we'll call Sven) walked over and asked him if he had seen the floating Volvo before. "Yeah, right," said Dave, "a floating Volvo." "No, really," Sven said, and went on to explain that they had been working on the technology for years and had finally brought it to market. And as soon as Sven figured out that Dave was indeed a buyer (the clipboard with the checkbook attached was probably the giveaway), he promptly suggested a test drive.

So Dave and Sven went out to the lot and, sure enough, there were several floating Volvos all set to go. They got into one and took it for a spin. Well, it handled great, was smooth and quiet, and had remarkable acceleration. Sven explained that the system was based on a revolutionary antigravity engine that they had designed and patented, and as such there were fewer moving parts and less friction, so the car stopped on a dime and had hardly any body roll when cornering. All in all, quite breathtaking.

Dave then asked the dreaded question, "So how much does it cost?" To Dave's great surprise, Sven told him that it was actually a little less than most of the standard Volvos—due to so many fewer moving parts. It was also much cheaper to maintain as, once again, fewer parts were subject to wear and tear.

When they get back to the showroom and after Sven had gone off to get some coffee, Dave thought about it for a while. And in the end, he decided to buy a nice silver S-80 sedan with the optional six-cylinder engine. Why? The floating Volvo was simply too good to be true. There seemed to be an implied risk in something so new, so innovative. There were many unanswered questions about the future of a floating car. It was just too radical. After all, Dave had gone shopping for a good car, not a new concept.

Sometimes you can offer your prospect just too much. Although your offering exceeds their needs, they are probably looking for something with which they are familiar. Perhaps the right way to sell the floating Volvo is to put wheels on it and keep quiet about its antigravity engine. If a prospect is

The Case of the Floating Volvo

interested in cost of ownership, you could stress the low gas mileage and overall reduced maintenance costs. If another prospect is interested in safety, we could talk about the great braking. And if another prospect is interested in performance, then let's show off the handling and acceleration.

And then maybe after the new owner (perhaps even Dave) is used to the new car and brings it back for service, the shop manager just may quietly mention, "You know, you can run that car without the wheels."

If you're selling a floating Volvo, you may want to put some wheels on it. Don't oversell your offering. Know what your prospects are looking for and what they value, and sell to those points.

5 Sales World

Show Your Stuff— by Asking Questions?

Sometimes we're just too anxious to demonstrate our expertise. Consider these two different sales calls to a vice president of manufacturing.

Jack, our first sales professional, walks in the door, and after a few minutes of small talk the real conversation starts. A couple of minutes in, the prospect mentions the challenges that he has been experiencing in quality control with a new assembly process. Jack sees an immediate opportunity to demonstrate his expertise and, springing up to the whiteboard, he starts to sketch out various practical and philosophical approaches to the whole matter of quality control. Being a true expert, he does not lack for subject matter. Soon, forty-five minutes have gone by and he is running out of time on his allotted one hour. And, as often happens, the end of the meeting is a little rushed as the prospect needs to prepare for another meeting. However, a few more pleasantries are exchanged and they thank each other for their time.

Jack considers this an excellent call, as he was really able to demonstrate his knowledge in the area and was even able to show how his own company's offerings differ from everyone else's.

Marion, our second sales professional, possesses some knowledge in the area of manufacturing but quite frankly probably can't hold a candle to Jack regarding subject matter.

She calls on this same prospect, but the conversation flows quite differently. After the usual small talk, she starts to ask questions. After each question she listens with an obvious and sincere interest and also takes a few notes. Questions build upon each other. The prospect doesn't at all feel that he is being interrogated and enjoys the opportunity to share his vision, challenges, and opportunities with an interested party. In fact a number of questions provoke a response of "great question" or "I hadn't thought of that." Some ten minutes prior to the end of the call, Marion wraps up by summarizing what she has learned. With time to spare, she closes the call by asking for a follow-up meeting to share ideas of how her company may be able to bring value to the prospect's organization in the areas that have been discussed. She gets his approval to do so and takes one last minute to schedule the next meeting.

Now, let's reflect on what has happened here.

In the first call, Jack did most of the talking. It is a fact that most people would rather talk than listen, so he enjoyed the call and he knows that he really got to strut his stuff. However, from the prospect's perspective, he likely wasn't expecting a sermon or a lecture even if it was passionately and enthusiastically delivered. It's a good bet that he was already aware of the philosophies espoused by Jack and might even have been a little bored. There is a good probability that he'll write off Jack as maybe too arrogant, a bit of a bore, and perhaps even a potential cause for concern in that he did not agree with some of Jack's points. What's more, Jack did not uncover or learn much about the prospect. Good call? You be the judge.

In the second call we see that Marion gained credibility by asking good questions. She let the prospect talk, demonstrated a sincere interest by doing the hard work, and showed the professionalism of good listening. It is likely that after the

Show Your Stuff—by Asking Questions?

meeting the prospect formed a very favorable opinion of her. Ironically, he would also likely consider that Marion knew more about his business than Jack did. After all, that is what the conversation with Marion was about: *his* business.

Unfortunately, I have been on far too many calls like the first—especially when I was with an enthusiastic and passionate expert. It is really quite amazing that afterwards, the reps think they have just had a great call, but the prospect is likely all too glad that the meeting was only an hour.

Demonstrate expertise and discover what is really happening in your prospect's world by asking great questions and listening.

Lights ... Camera ... Action!

Now, there's a well-known expression, and so often used as a metaphor in so many ways. And the common thread among all its various usages is the implication that after extensive preparation, something special is about to happen. If we delve deeper into the actual activity behind the scenes on a movie set, we can see why something special does indeed happen when the director makes the call.

Lights—and think of all the preparation that must happen before the lights are even turned on. From knowledge and research, the screenwriter, the set designer, and many others all work together to build a compelling story with words, sets, and costumes. And only then can the lighting designer determine how to fulfill the director's needs with a vast array of light and color to enhance the mood and ambiance—to bring to light and illuminate the story.

Camera—the director of photography is now often regarded as the second most important person on the set. His or her mastery of craft and equipment is the funnel through which the story travels from the studio to the screen. But without a story, a set design, or lighting, the best cinematographer in the business wouldn't come up with much. And when you think of it, the real job of the camera is to be focused and pointing in the right direction.

Action—something special happens! Hours and hours of preparation have paid off, if only for a few minutes of actual action. What have all these people been doing?

Lights ... Camera ... Action!

Getting prepared. And that's exactly how a sales call has to be.

When I am working with sales folk, one of the most important areas we work on is how to turn a sales call from the standard product pitch into a valuable and rewarding interaction with our prospects wherein we discover as much as we can about their specific needs and wants. There is no question in the minds of these sales professionals just how important this is—the need to understand what their prospects are looking for, what their priorities are, and what various alternatives they may be considering. The challenge, however, is how to show up, ask questions, and start listening—not pitching. And I recall one particular situation that really underscores this challenge.

I was working with Trish, a very accomplished and successful salesperson. Through a contact of hers she had managed to set up a first call with the local general manager of a large organization. This was actually quite a coup and a situation that wouldn't come along every day, as this company spent considerable money with one of our competitors. However, we also knew they had some new business challenges in an area where we certainly could help, so we really wanted to make this meeting count.

We turned up ten minutes early for the call and at the appointed time we were collected by our prospect's executive assistant from reception and shown the way to a large corner office on the top floor. There we were greeted by a larger-than-life character (straight out of the movies, you could almost say—the office certainly was) who ushered us into his office. He sat behind his desk (again of Hollywood proportions) and we dutifully took seats on the other side of what seemed like a football field. And everything was very cordial; small talk about the weather, and him offering and us accepting coffee and tea.

Then it was time to get down to business and it didn't take much skill to recognize this, as he cued us very efficiently. "So, thank you for taking the time to come by, and tell me—what have you got for me today?"

There it was—the invitation to go into sales presentation mode. That was what he was expecting and that is exactly what would have been so easy to do. We could have started talking about all our wonderful products and services, all of the wonderful things we could do, and all of the wonderful things that make us special. Trouble is, that would likely have achieved precisely nothing. We would have left the meeting with little or no understanding of his business, his priorities, or his goals or needs.

The challenge is—when you are faced with that invitation, how do you respond?

This was our moment of action. But as the expression goes, lights and camera come before action. You have to prepare for this moment. If you have no knowledge about the customer or the situation, you will have few alternatives when it comes to action but to go into your standard sales pitch. What we have to do is to prepare for the action.

Lights are illuminating and learning. Learning all you can about the prospects and their situations. We talked earlier about the knowledge and research involved on the movie set—well, no different here. And to expand on another story in this book, this is where the Internet really comes into its own. Information that once took hours to discover can now be gained in minutes. Before any call to a new prospect or even with existing customers, you should always research and find out all you can—what's important to them, what's new for them. The Internet can yield vast quantities of information about a company, its financial health, its competition, the industry trends it faces, new appointments, and the latest things that it considers newsworthy.

Lights ... Camera ... Action!

If you're calling on a senior executive, try running his or her name through Google. As an aside, I once Googled a prospect of mine only to discover that, among other things, he and his family gave a testimonial for a new type of construction material. There they were on the net, talking about what a great time they had had rebuilding their house with this particular construction company. So what, you may ask? Well, I learned all about their family, including the dog, and when I walked in to that first meeting it was far from being a cold call.

Camera—and remember the movie set; the camera must be focused and pointing in the right direction. And in the world of sales we do that with the call plan. Before every sales call we should always take the time to think about what it is we are trying to achieve and how are we going to change the course of events as a result of this meeting. The call plan has to focus on these goals and should prepare us for what challenges, objections, or issues may arise. And most importantly, we should carefully plan the questions we want to ask.

We are now prepared for real action here. We know what information we'd really like to discover. We've given thought to what issues are likely to be on the mind of our prospect. And armed with knowledge, we'll have the ability to demonstrate our unique capabilities by sharing how we have helped others in similar situations.

And after learning all we can about the situation, we have developed a call plan that will give us focus and direction and enable us to maximize the use of our time with the prospect. We are prepared for action. We are ready to make something special happen!

Action—the action happens when, instead of dropping into sales pitch mode, we bring to bear all the preparation that we've done. We utilize the knowledge and information we have gleaned prior to the call by asking insightful questions and listening carefully to the responses they bring about. We follow our call plan to ensure that all aspects of the customer's situation are thoroughly examined. The plan we follow, the questions we ask, and the answers we receive will then enable us to propose a unique solution to help them achieve their specific business goals.

When faced with a situation similar to that Trish and I found ourselves in, the table has to be turned. Our call plan should prepare us to ask questions that will engage our prospect in the conversation. As most people would rather talk than listen, you will more than likely discover that your customer is only too willing, when cued appropriately, to take over the conversation. This doesn't mean that you have to remain silent about all the great things you have to offer. When the time is right, you can (and should) share these in a concise and meaningful way.

Let's get back to our story. When it came time for Trish's action, the learning and call planning paid off. Rather than reacting like the proverbial deer in the headlights when faced with a prospect who says "Well, what have you got for me today?" and falling into a standard sales pitch, Trish was able to handle the situation as a true sales professional.

"Well, first of all, we would like to thank you for your time today. We know that you must be very busy with the acquisition of the ABC company. That is a very interesting strategy for you, and we assume that it will give you access to new markets. It would be great if you could spend a few minutes and share with us how you intend to leverage this."

Not expecting this, he was obviously impressed that we weren't there to waste his time; we were prepared and had opened up a conversation that was topical and relevant to him. He shared the background of the merger with us, what he thought the challenges and the opportunities would be. Trish continued to use her knowledge of the situation, and followed the call plan to steer the conversation into areas that we believed that we could provide valuable assistance.

We left the meeting an hour later after developing a significantly deeper understanding of the company and where we might be able to help. We did not pitch our products or services, but rather discussed how our capabilities might be able to help him achieve some of his goals more quickly. We confirmed his interest, and set the date for a further meeting where we would review a proposal with him of exactly how we could help in his own specific situation. Needless to say, Trish was well on her way to gaining his trust and business.

And just like the traditional Hollywood ending ... the scene opens three months later, and the camera pans onto a smiling Trish with a signed contract in her hand.

Sales mastery comes from asking insightful questions. To achieve this mastery when it comes time for action, be prepared by learning all you can about the prospect, and develop the confidence that comes from comprehensive call planning.

Lights—Illuminate your subject by learning all you can about the prospect.

Camera—Be focused and pointing in the right direction with your call plan.

Action—Ask insightful questions, listen, and make something special happen.

When a Pencil Is More Than a Pencil

When we conduct sales workshops, we often put writing pads and pencils on the tables for all of our participants. We buy these "no-name" pencils in one of the big office stores for around seventy cents each. You know the type—they often come in packs of three, complete with several lead refills that can be replaced and an eraser on the blunt end. I know you can replenish the leads because I buy the refills and use them in both the no-name pencils and in my Mont Blanc pencil. Which gets me thinking.

My wife gave me my Mont Blanc as a gift a few years ago and it is undoubtedly a lovely writing instrument. However, I was thinking that I use exactly the same lead refill in both the no-name pencil and the Mont Blanc. So aside from the obvious $116.29 price spread, what's the difference? I could get 140 of those pencils for the price of the Mont Blanc.

So let's do a quick feature-to-feature comparison and see how they really stack up.

When a Pencil Is More Than a Pencil

	No-name	Mont Blanc	Advantage
Writing ability	Same lead	Same lead	Equal
Ease of use	Eraser always available	Eraser under cover	No-name
Color choice	Many colors	Three colors	No-name
Availability	Every office store	Selected stores	No-name
Usability	Take it anywhere, give it away, no concern if you lose it.	Fear of being lost or stolen; hate to lend it to anyone.	No-name
Replacement price	Seventy cents	$117	No-name
Storage ability	Has pocket clip	Has pocket clip	Equal

As a result of this objective feature-to-feature comparison, there is no doubt that we can declare the no-name pencil the winner. But wait a minute; why is the Mont Blanc 150 times the cost and how can that possibly be justified? And furthermore, why do you see such a significant number of people using a Mont Blanc?

Let's apply this analogy to our day-to-day work. Have you ever been in a situation where you were selling the equivalent of the Mont Blanc, and your prospect arrived at the same objective decision that we've outlined above, unable to believe how much your product or service costs?

And conversely, have you ever been selling the equivalent

of the no-name pencil and been totally mystified at how your prospect totally disregarded your cost-effective and compelling proposal only to purchase a much more costly offering?

I have, and both ways.

So what is going on here? Well, let's just add one more line to our analysis.

	No-name	Mont Blanc	Advantage
Prestige	Zero	Lots	It depends

There is a distinct prestige factor associated with owning a Mont Blanc. I am sure that the Mont Blanc people themselves will not only persuasively argue that their pencil represents a finely crafted tool—which translates into a certain pride of ownership—but they may even try to make the case that it will be easier to use, is better balanced, has that certain "feel," all of which will result in a better writing experience. Could be, I suppose, but in the end it really depends on what the buyer wants. Unlike price, where we can definitively say that the no-name pencil has the advantage, it totally depends on what the buyer is looking for: what the buyer *values*.

When my wife visited the store to buy that gift, I trust that no matter how persuasive a salesperson she may have encountered, I would not—hopefully—have ended up with a three-pack of no-name pencils for Christmas. She was looking for a gift that would have special attributes that she knew I would appreciate and value.

The same applies the other way around. I doubt that you will find Mont Blanc pencils in front of you any day soon at one of our seminars. When shopping for these, I am looking to buy a large number of pencils that are reliable and inexpensive.

When a Pencil Is More Than a Pencil

Different expectations, different requirements, and different values.

Although these two items are very definitely pencils, they represent two vastly different value propositions. And remember, the key here is that the value is relevant only when it is of value to the buyer.

To be successful in our selling efforts, we must understand what each individual prospect values, and then sell our offering to match that specific value.

Do You Know Why Someone Will Buy from You?

A while back, I was sitting in on a simulated loss review for a large strategic sales opportunity. For those of you who may not be familiar with this process, a simulated loss review is conducted toward the end of the sales process—usually immediately prior to the submission of the proposal or presentation of the offering. Essentially the members of the selling team get together and project themselves into the future to a specific date immediately after the prospect has made their decision to either buy from us or take an alternate route—perhaps to go with a competitive offering, to delay, to do nothing, or do something internally within its organization.

The objective of this process is to pretend that you have lost the business, and then try to understand the most likely reasons for such a loss and carefully examine all the aspects of the sale that could have been done differently. Hopefully, and most importantly, it is then not too late to change the selling approach to prevent the envisioned loss.

In this particular instance we were competing once again with IBM. The session had been going well for several hours, but then a startling and unsettling discovery was made when we simulated a phone call from Bill, the prospective client, to Jessica, the account manager for our team, and it went something like this:

Do You Know Why Someone Will Buy from You?

"Hi, Jessica, Bill here. As you know, we met with our steering committee yesterday to look at your proposal and make a decision on which way to go. Unfortunately, I don't have good news for you, but I wanted to share this with you personally. We have decided to go with IBM and I will be informing them of our decision over lunch today. I wanted to thank you and your team for all the work you did putting your proposal together for us, and we really appreciate the time you took to understand our needs. I would look forward to getting together with you in the future and wish you continued success in your career."

Ouch! This won't work—this is not what Jessica wants to hear. She's thinking, "Bill, if you're really concerned about my successful career, you'll give us this business!" Panic strikes, but it's not lunchtime yet—maybe there is still a chance. He'll listen—we've both invested significantly in this relationship over the past six months. But we also know we'll only have a few minutes to make our point. What do we say?

At this point we stumbled. We had lots of detail, lots of information, and a great deal of confidence that we were presenting a better solution for the business. But how do you nail all that down in sixty seconds? We realized that we had become so caught up in the details, dealing with so many trees, that we lost sight of the big forest right in front of our eyes. We could not say—in simple and straightforward language—why Bill should buy from us.

Well, we sent out for pizza and lots of midnight oil and stayed in that meeting room until late that evening. We went back through all of our research and information to formulate a clear and compelling reason why Bill should buy from us over any alternative. We then condensed, edited, and polished that information so that we could express it in not only a few words but, just as importantly, in *Bill's* words. From that point forward, we ensured that all of our proposals and presentations included this compelling reason to buy, our *value proposition*, in a very clear and concise manner.

Jessica never did get that phone call, and we did win the business.

Remember—if you don't know why the prospect would buy from you, don't expect the prospect to know.

Companies Fund, People Buy

In sitting through account planning and sales strategy sessions, we often absorb a lot of great information about the prospective client company. We can discuss the state of their business, what their challenges are, what they are looking for, and what the competitors are doing, to name just a few. With all this information about them, it is then assumed that we have all the required information to put together a winning sales strategy.

Now, this is not to denigrate that information; it is all vital and necessary to better understand our target prospect. But in focusing on it we far too often overlook an important fact: it is not the company that buys, it is a person—an individual or a network of individuals. And these are individuals with their own personal concerns, motivations, anxieties, and personal goals. Any and all buying decisions must ultimately come down to people somewhere saying "yes."

In any selling situation we must place an emphasis on not only understanding the organizational situation of our prospect but also the individual motivations, desires, and fears of each and every person that will be making or influencing the decision.

Just because an offering is right for the company doesn't mean that it is right for the individual. Find out who those individuals are, determine their needs and desires, and tailor your approach to them. And remember: companies fund, people buy.

Finding Value Finds Customers

The great marketing guru Theodore Levitt wrote in the seventies that "there is no such thing as a commodity." Perhaps in today's fast-paced, shrink-wrapped world where it's become increasingly difficult to protect any competitive advantage, it would seem that this notion has become somewhat outdated. With automated reverse engineering and shop floor robotics allowing the "me-too" crowd to quickly overhaul the "me-first" entrepreneurs with similar and cheaper products, aided and abetted by mass merchandising and online stores, it sometimes seems that our whole world has been commoditized. However, I happen to think Levitt was, and indeed still is, correct.

Let's take the example of an envelope—a regular business-style envelope. On the surface, what could be more generic than an envelope? The choice is usually limited to size, with or without a window, and white or manila—sounds like a commodity to me. So why wouldn't companies simply buy envelopes from whoever can supply them the cheapest? Well, I suppose a lot do, but interestingly enough there is one particular company that charges more, makes more profit, and owns the majority of that market share.

This particular company—let's call it ABC—tends to do things differently. Most other envelope providers wait for the purchasing department of a company to issue an RFP and then try to beat the competition in price for the business.

Let's take the real case of where the salesperson for ABC approached a major airline.

Finding Value Finds Customers

ABC Salesperson: So, can you tell me how you use envelopes?

Airline Person: What?

ABC Salesperson: Can you tell me how you use envelopes?

Airline Person: Well, what do you think—we put stuff in them, put a stamp on them, and then mail them.

ABC Salesperson: OK, great, but how do you really use the envelope?

Airline Person: Well, I guess there really isn't much more to it than what I just told you.

ABC Salesperson: You know, we often find that companies have no idea how much they are paying for envelopes and how they could get more from that investment. Would you mind if we took a look at this for you?

Airline Person: Go for it—I'm sure you'll find it very interesting.

Over the next week or so, a couple of folk from ABC took a closer look at how much that airline was spending on envelopes and what it used them for. They discovered that the second highest use of envelopes was for sending frequent-flyer statements out every month. At the next meeting with Airline Person, the following conversation took place.

ABC Salesperson: Were you aware that your second largest use of envelopes is to send out monthly statements to your frequent flyers?

Airline Person: Well, now that you mention it, that doesn't surprise me.

ABC Salesperson: In fact, you spend $$$s on those envelopes every month.

Airline Person: Really—that much?

ABC Salesperson: Yes, that much—but of course it all depends on what you are getting back on that money. It's interesting that from a marketing point of view, frequent flyers must be one of your most important markets, and yet every month you communicate with them by sending them a basic white envelope. Our research would show that more than 74 percent of those envelopes never even get opened. What if we were able to design an envelope for you that would allow you to present a personalized message on the outside, perhaps showing how many more flights the customer needed to reach the next status level, or offering special fares—aimed at their specific location and travel profiles? What if we could get twice as many people to open the envelope and then twice as many people to respond to those special offers? If we could work with you to design that envelope that would communicate the right message, what would that be worth to you?

Airline Person: Wow—I never thought of it that way.

Guess who now supplies all the envelopes to that airline. They no longer send out RFPs to envelope suppliers to see who can offer them the cheapest. They now have a partner that works with them to understand how they can use envelopes in more interesting, innovative, and profitable ways.

Don't always accept that your offering is generic or commoditized. Search for where you can deliver unique value to your customer, and by finding value you will find customers.

Yours Sincerely

For those of us who are old enough to remember the days of typewriters and mailed letters—before the days of personal computers and e-mail—you may recall that we signed off most of those letters with "yours sincerely." Business letter writing, which included just about all written communication with clients, prospects, and partners, was certainly more formal than today's e-mail and instant messaging. And yes, there were many other differences as well, but it wasn't so long ago that rather than tapping out a quick e-mail, more time, and I would suggest more care, was taken in composing these communications. I learned my lesson this way.

I was out one day with Ken, the president of the company I worked for, and we had just had a successful meeting with a prospect. Upon returning to the office he suggested it would be a good idea to write a letter thanking the prospect for her time and reiterating the points of our proposal that we considered compelling. Good idea, I thought, and we sat down for what I thought would be a few minutes to fire off a nice note to the prospect.

Imagine my surprise when it took an hour and a half just to rough out three short paragraphs. I sat there adding my own input as Ken first drafted the objectives for the letter and then outlined each paragraph. More time than I thought imaginable was dedicated to choosing exactly the right words to describe our value proposition to the prospect. Sentences were tried and revised with various phrases to evaluate which best articulated the points we wanted to make. Paragraphs were written, read, and then read again to see if they actually said what we meant to say.

Even then the process was not complete. When the completed draft was written, Ken then surprised me again and suggested we sleep on it and return to do a final revision in the morning. I guess at that moment my surprise and perhaps my impatience were showing, and so he then shared with me a value that many years later still guides my own style. He said if it's worth writing, it's worth writing properly. At the end of every memo, letter, or indeed e-mail you write, you add your name. It doesn't really matter what closing salutation you use; at the end it is always your name. It used to be your signature, but even today, any communication ends with your name.

So does that e-mail represent you as you wish to be seen? Is it clear and concise? Does it read as you wish it to be read? Is there any possible ambiguity or potential cause for misinterpretation? There's a good chance that at one time or another we've all been responsible for writing something that has been taken the wrong way. I have no doubt that a little more care and attention in the writing would prevent almost all of those misunderstandings and, in doing so, preclude the effort and cost that so often go along with such mistakes.

When you sign your name at the end of an e-mail, letter, or memo, does that document represent you as you wish to be seen? After all, it's your name.

The Large Account Management Paradox

For many salespeople, large account management is much preferred over selling to numerous smaller accounts. I have heard many salespeople say that they just don't like the prospecting that comes with a general territory and much prefer to manage a handful of large clients. Of course this is only natural—the chance to make a few big scores always seems a much more valuable (and enjoyable) investment of time than having to peg away day after day on the little deals.

With these large clients, however, there are invariably many activities demanding the sales professional's time—activities that would genuinely seem to come under the general heading of account management. These activities are often associated with post-sales follow-up and checking on delivery. They often involve chasing paperwork, ensuring that rollouts are happening as expected, and keeping the client up to date with all that is new and wonderful. As the salesperson gets to know and be comfortable with the account, there are often more people to interface with about more things. This often results in building and managing relationships with many individuals spanning from purchasing through finance, and obviously the end users themselves. Now, this is a good thing; in fact, it could be said that this is what good account management is all about, but it is important to remember that relationships consume a lot of time and energy and an eye must always be kept out to ensure that it is time well spent.

The problem I've seen rise again and again is that this activity starts to take an ever-increasing percentage of the week. As a sales manager, I have often heard sales folk on my team share with me that they are going to "just go and call on Jack Smith at XYZ Corp. to keep him up to speed," or "I'll be upstairs in contracts getting some details ironed out with that deal from last week." All legitimate-sounding things to do, but there is a very real danger that these meetings aren't really serving any useful purpose to us as salespeople. It is undeniably important to leverage your external contacts and it never hurts to make sure that your internal processes are running smoothly, but there are two dangerous traps that I see large-account salespeople fall into.

The first trap is that the salesperson becomes far too involved in the post-sales aspects of their accounts. He or she becomes the go-to person, and in extreme cases the sales rep becomes the go-to person for both the client's people *and* his or her own people.

When Jim—our major account manager—is with his client, he may start to hear such things as:

"Hey, Jim, when are those call center systems going to show up?"

"Jim, could you look into this invoice for us? It doesn't seem to be right."

"Can we get an extra copy of that statement, Jim?"

And then when he's in his own office, it's:

"Jim, XYZ Corp. ordered ten systems but we've only got six. Is it okay to send those out today, and the rest next week?"

"Is this still the right shipping address for XYZ Corp.?"

"Jim, do you know the right tax code for these people?"

Funny thing is, all of these questions would still be asked of smaller clients and indeed get answered *without a salesperson's*

The Large Account Management Paradox

involvement. And unfortunately, the more Jim takes on these issues, the more they will just keep on coming. In the worst situations, both organizations start to rely on Jim to become the progress chaser, project manager, delivery expert, and hand-holder for all issues and problems.

The second trap is when the salesperson is spending the bulk of his or her time on these aforementioned "account management" activities and spending less and less time looking for new business. Unless the salesperson is in the very fortunate (and unlikely) position where:

» the business she has already secured from her large accounts will make her quotas,

» *and* there is absolutely no more business to be had from these accounts,

» *and* there is no competitive activity or threat of competitive activity in the accounts,

... *then there are new sales to be made!*

And if there are sales to be made, there is prospecting to do.

The nature of undertaking new business development—*prospecting*—within an existing client is not all that different from that in a "cold" territory. And when you think about it, prospecting within a large account that you're familiar with should be a lot easier and a lot less threatening than cold calling, right? Just have your buddy Jack in purchasing introduce you to the IT manager or get the names of the HR people and pop up and see them. Unfortunately, easier and more often said than done.

Take the case of Susan, who managed a large account for me at one time and was very busy with all of her account management activities. Month after month her sales reports showed that she was knowledgeable about her client and was managing the existing opportunities well. Her sales were growing quarterly by some 15 percent, and we were seeing $300,000 to $400,000 of business each quarter. Good account management, you may think, until one day the competition announced a $1.4 million order from the same client—*and we didn't even know the opportunity existed!* Sue had spent all of her valuable selling time meeting with her existing contacts, making sure that everything (that she was aware of) was going well.

Don't get tangled up in the Large Account Paradox—treat it like a territory. Leverage your client knowledge and internal contacts and always be searching for new contacts and new opportunities.

Are Objections Objectionable?

I don't have the time right now.
    We don't have the budget.
    I need to get others involved.
    This is a busy time of year.
    We'll have to think it over and get back to you.

Heard that before? These and seemingly countless others are typical objections that are part of every sales professional's day. And we know all too well that such objections can potentially ruin an otherwise great sales effort. However, there are a number of interesting facts—six to be precise—that we should know about objections.

For many years now, usually as part of comprehensive sales seminars, I've conducted workshops on how to handle objections. We start the workshop by asking the participants to break into small groups and list all—and I mean all—of the objections they have ever heard or are ever likely to hear. Almost invariably the moaning starts and they ask how they could possibly list them all—to which we reply that they should then list as many as they can in the time available. We usually introduce this workshop right before lunch, as this allows everyone time to collect their thoughts, and the groups wander off to eat, anticipating that they will be working at coming up with literally hundreds of objections. After lunch we get down to work, and then a strange thing happens—which brings me to fact #1 about objections.

Sales World

Fact #1: There are far fewer actual objections than we think.

On writing down the list of all likely objections, we first find that there are rarely more than twenty or so in total. We then take a closer look and see how many of those cited are in actual fact duplications, or near enough that we can cull the list further. And then we do a reality check to see if all the objections we have come across in real life are all there—and indeed they usually are. Not the hundreds anticipated—closer perhaps to a couple of dozen or so.

Fact #2: Most objections could be avoided by gaining a better understanding of the situation earlier in the sales cycle.

With the final list of objections posted, we work on what to do when we hear them. What we discover is that the majority could have been prevented if we had just thought to ask a few more questions and discover a bit more about our prospect earlier in the sales cycle:

Is there a budget for this project?

Who will be involved in the decision-making process, and what will it be?

Are you considering alternative approaches?

What are the major factors that you will be considering?

Who else should I be talking to?

If we asked these questions, and any others that are relevant, the majority of likely objections would melt away. Which is a lot better than the melting away of a lot of work that was invested in the sales effort only to discover key information gaps that surface as—you guessed it—objections.

Fact #3: Some objections are phantoms, inasmuch as they are simply convenient ways to block the truth.

When we study the remaining objections, we will often find that they are not real—what I choose to call "phantom" objections. It is far easier for prospects to tell you that they

Are Objections Objectionable?

would like to think about your proposal for a while than to admit that they do not have the budget, or they lack the authority to proceed, or any other genuine but internal, and therefore private, business matters. Phantoms can also arise for seemingly nonrelevant issues; maybe they don't like your style, or they're going through some personal difficulties. These might seem tough to see through, but if Fact #2 has been dealt with, it's a fair assumption that some phantoms are flying.

Now, let's take a little time-out from the fact list. If we look at all of the objections, take away the ones that could have been prevented by better discovery, and take away the phantoms, we are left with a much smaller list to manage. From these—*which invariably represent the real business objections to our proposals*—we can take a far more positive view of the situation because we have a manageable, solvable, and informative list to deal with. Why informative? Read on.

Fact #4: Real objections are a buying signal. If we've persevered and dispensed with the "unreal" objections, chances are that both of us—the sales professional and the purchaser—have invested a good deal of time and energy into the process. Most objections we hear at this stage should be representing the genuine needs and anxieties of our prospect, and they would not be shared if there weren't a serious interest in buying.

Fact #5: Often the real motivations (and fears) only come out through objections.

It is at this stage of the selling cycle that we often hear the real emotional needs of our prospect. Up to this point, the sales cycle may have been totally founded upon business needs involving clear and objective requirements. It is here when we may hear things such as, "But isn't your company likely to be acquired? What happens then?" Or, "I'm really not sure if we're ready to do business with a company that is still in its infancy." These are the real objections that are not raised earlier but often represent true issues that need to be dealt with.

So what have we learned?

Fact #6: Most objections are predictable.

Objections really are wonderful things because they impart information. And when we look back with hindsight on both deals that we won and deals that went south, we find that virtually all of the objections were totally predictable. And if most objections are indeed predictable, we should be able to list them, be prepared and confident to deal with them, and learn from them.

Objections need not be objectionable. Compile your own list of the objections you are likely to hear. Look to see which could have been avoided, and then make sure that you can respond to the ones remaining—the real ones—with confidence and competence.

The Price Is Too High—Oh, Really?

Oh, the confusion, angst, and general hand-wringing with this simple statement! And followed all too often with a knee-jerk rush to discount. The prospect says the price is too high—but is it really?

I used to drive BMWs. When choosing a new one, I would always haggle a little over the price—it made me feel good. The last thing I wanted when I left the showroom was the sales reps doing high-fives, celebrating the first time they had ever sold a car at 5 percent over list price. No one likes to leave money on the table and most of us like to think we have gotten a good deal. But when you think about it, if price really mattered in the overall equation, what the heck was I doing buying a BMW?

Price is the simplest and probably the most common form of objection. However, most of us know that saying the price is too high usually disguises all sorts of *real* objections. The truth most likely lies in something quite different. Some things such as:

I don't have the authority to buy.
We don't have the budget.
I haven't discussed this with my boss yet.
I want to look at the competition.
I'm not sure that you can deliver what you say.
I don't know if we really need this now.
We have other priorities right now.

If a prospect really wants to wriggle out of any sort of commitment with a salesperson, it's just so easy and gives away far less to say the price is too high.

However, the good sales professional, we must assume, has done his or her homework and has already addressed the points that I've listed. Perhaps the issue here is that we have not *translated* our benefits into a language or format that the prospect either understands or is comfortable with. So if we agree that price is not really the issue, maybe what the prospect is saying is, "The value is too low."

We have to look at a different equation than price—we have to look at *value*. And not only must we look at value, we must quantify it and what it means to our prospects, and put it into terms that the prospects will understand. What will our prospects gain as a result of investing in our offering and how do they personally value that? When buying that BMW, I believed I was investing in great engineering, a car that I enjoyed driving, and doubtless a modest amount of prestige. My wife, on the other hand, places little value on these aspects of a car and wondered why I was prepared to pay double or triple what she pays for a car that she thinks is superior, due to her preferences like cost of ownership and high resale price—things she *values*.

When we are selling any product or service we have to know what value it will deliver to our prospect and not, I must stress, the value we see. And it must not only be the value the customers see, but also be presented in terms that they will understand and be comfortable with. The key question to be answered then is, does that value outweigh all of the costs of investment? And on the cost side it's not just the purchase price—we must also consider the total cost of ownership, which can often include any fears, doubts, and uncertainties that our prospect may have. They must believe (or perceive) that the value of our offering is higher than the cost of acquisition.

The Price Is Too High—Oh, Really?

Price all by itself can never be "too high"—it has to be relative to something. Make sure that in the mind of the customer, the value of your offering outweighs the costs.

So What?

I was involved with a proposal to an organization that we hoped would become a very significant new client. A lot of time and energy had been invested in writing a professional-looking proposal. As I read the draft document I could appreciate the effort that it must have taken. A good overview of our company was given, followed by a comprehensive description of our proposed products and services. The document read well, but I was worried that it lacked a certain amount of selling punch.

I then recalled an old trick I had picked up earlier in my career. At the end of every paragraph I'd take a red pen and write "so what?" and then see if the document, statement, paragraph, etc. had answered that question from the prospect's perspective.

One might see something like this in a proposal.

"Our company was founded in 1974 and now employs more than 35,000 people in sixteen centers across the country. We service more than 1,000 clients from twenty-six world-class service centers. In 1999 we became ISO 9000 certified, and we won the Malcolm Baldridge Excellence Award in 2001."

So what?

Exactly—so what. And assume that the prospects are going to ask it themselves, even if only subconsciously. Try this; quite often a good segue from one of these open-ended paragraphs or statements would start with "What this means

So What?

to you is ..." or "Because of this ..." and then a bridge that refers back to issues or concerns that the prospect has made you aware of. So now let's answer "so what?" from the prospect's perspective. This may include such things as:

» "What this means to you is that we have the proven ability to provide you with the service you need to ensure that your plants are kept running 24/7."

» "Because of this we can provide a consistently high level of reliable service to you at each of your locations across the country."

» "You stated in your RFP that service was a major concern; our proven track record demonstrates that you can rely on us to meet or exceed your exacting service requirements."

Whatever it may be, we must specifically reply to "so what?" for every statement we make. We cannot rely upon the prospects to read our great claims and then immediately and automatically translate them into what it means for them.

This great two-word test not only works for writing, but also speaking. The next time you prepare a presentation, take a look and see if you are indeed answering "so what?" for each point that you intend to make.

Every time you write, present, or speak to your prospect, make sure that you answer the question "so what?" clearly, directly, and from the prospect's point of view.

The Difference between Interest and Commitment

How many times have you been faced with a salesperson selling to you? Perhaps it's happened at a trade show, in the course of your business, or even in a social environment. And however you may have arrived at the situation, there you are with a salesperson taking a run at you.

They are obviously enthusiastic about what they are pitching, seem to know what they're talking about, and often have nice glossy brochures to back up their verbal assault. Most of us are relatively social and empathetic to a degree, and so what do we say? Well, usually nice nonthreatening things like "sounds interesting" or "let me think about it." These are also safe words. If we choose to say what we really feel, like "I haven't a clue what you are talking about," or "Yeah, yeah, you and a thousand others," or "Not a chance—too expensive," you risk being either bombarded by more enthusiastic claims and explanations or offending a probably nice person who just caught you at the wrong time. Safe harbor can be found in "sounds interesting" or "leave it with me, I will give it some thought."

And so ends the dialogue—you likely junk the brochure and never give it another moment's thought. But what has often inadvertently happened here is—to the ear of the salesperson anyway—we have expressed *interest*. And to the enthusiastic true believer of the sales credo, *interest begets com-*

The Difference between Interest and Commitment

mitment. And many salespeople will leave that conversation having noted your interest and will list you as a prospect.

I have seen so many salespeople mistake the words and signals of interest as strong buying signals. There can be many reasons that someone shows interest, real or feigned. I gave an example of one such reason above, and people will show signs of interest for any number of other reasons.

Exploration

Many people like to explore and see what is out there. They may be inquiring about your products or services for sometime in the future, or comparing them to something they already have. They may be stealing, borrowing, appropriating ideas from you for whatever reason, or simply educating themselves about what is going on. Ask any car salesman and he'll tell you there is no shortage of tire-kickers.

Not wishing to look stupid

I worked with a company that had crafted a very clever—even intellectual—presentation of its company and approaches. The executive who was presenting the pitch to various prospects assured me that people nodded and showed great interest. However, when we dug a little deeper, we found that most people had no idea what the message was, found the bulk of the presentation indecipherable, and just didn't want to look stupid.

Timing and circumstance

Even if we have prospects who are genuinely interested in our company or offering, do they have the ability to commit? Do they have the necessary funds and resources, are they empowered by the organization to make such a decision, and if so, when can they actually move forward?

Marketing vs. sales

I have also seen similar confusion regarding the difference between interest and commitment in marketing departments. Sitting in board meetings, I have heard marketing VPs reporting on how successful various campaigns have been due to the interest they have generated. Except that this interest is often measured by how many requests have been received for more information, how many brochures have been handed out at a trade show, or how many downloads have been requested from a Web site. Once again this level of interest generation, especially if it is the objective of the campaign, is good. However, from a sales standpoint, there is often little correlation between interest and commitment.

Now, I don't want to leave the impression that generating interest is not important—far from it. It is vital to a successful sales campaign. There can, however, be a very large gap between interest and commitment. After all, interest costs little, can be great fun, and is often illuminating. Commitment is work—from both sides of the transaction—and it doesn't come cheaply.

Although interest in your offering is very important, do not mistake interest for commitment. Interest comes in many shapes and sizes—commitment comes in the shape of a signed contract or purchase order.

What You Know ...
and What They Want

Several years ago, I finally gave in and decided to buy a DVD player. I am a little more cautious than I used to be about embracing new technology (I actually have a Betamax somewhere that still works, but there's not much to play on it—questionable track record, I know). At any rate, I figured I would go out to one of the many home stereo/electronics stores, pay about $250, and walk away with a new DVD.

So I put aside some time one Saturday morning and ventured down to the local mall and found a likely (and very big) store. Now, like many, I often find the salespeople in these places can be little more than a nuisance. And shortly after walking in and getting my bearings, I suffered the usual confrontation. I was just starting to look at what they had in stock, and up walks the "sales consultant" with an offer of assistance. He could see that I was looking at DVD players, so his form of assistance was to show me the two models that were on special. He took a deep breath, and away he went.

"Now, this first one's a beauty—multi-playback utility for CD, VCD, SVCD, DVD-Video, MP3, and JPEG. High-quality 12bit/128MHz video and an absolute killer 24bit/212KHz audio synchronizer. Composite, S-video, and DVD component outputs, DTS digital audio output, and precise drive mechanism with dynamic scan compensation. I think you'd have to agree that it's a sweet thing for the money. And this other one—

Sales World

wow—has all of those features plus dynamic laser actuator control and hi-res conducer. I don't know how the boss stays in business at these prices. Gotta buy today, though—the special's over when we close at six."

Well, I wondered how his boss stayed in business too, and not just because of the prices. And I found this both frustrating as a consumer, and saddening as someone who believes in true sales skills. If this was selling, then I was out of a job. But I'm not out of a job and this was not selling. I walked out of the store without buying, and somewhat disappointed.

A few weeks later I found myself in a shopping center with a few minutes to spare and there was yet another of these electronic toy stores. In I walked. Once again, as soon as I started looking at the display units of DVD players, a salesperson walked over.

"Good afternoon. I see you are looking at DVD players."

To which I responded with a barely civil "Yes."

"Can I offer you any help?"

"No, I'm okay, thanks, just going to have a look."

"Well, we have quite a range; perhaps I can help you narrow down your search."

"No, that's okay—just looking."

"Well, please feel free. May I ask what your main interest is in buying a DVD, and perhaps what other equipment you'll be hooking it up to?"

I soon found I was engaged in a conversation. Through our dialogue, the salesperson discovered that I was primarily interested in watching movies, and intended to hook up the player to my existing system. He also found out that I was quite interested in music, and as part of this hobby had actually designed and built my own speakers on my stereo system. He also discovered that I had quite an old television set. Now, true, it was color, but it was so incredibly old that it was not even equipped with a remote control—a fact that

What You Know ... and What They Want

always amazed my wife, as we were at that time a "remote-less" couple.

Without succumbing to what would have been reasonably justified smart remarks, he said, "Well, that's really too bad, especially considering your interest in music and obvious appreciation of quality sound. The audio from even the least expensive of DVD players won't be truly realized through the small speakers in your old television. In fact even the picture quality would leave something to be desired as well. And I suppose there could also be some connection issues." And I wasn't offended at all, as this was delivered sincerely and with an obvious desire to help.

As our conversation continued, I became interested in the latest advances in home entertainment. Although I used to be up on all the latest developments, I had fallen sadly behind the times. I had heard of many of the terms, but really didn't know what they all meant.

By this time, my knowledgeable salesperson knew the size of the room where the television was, and knew what my likes and dislikes were in terms of movies and music. He asked if I would be interested in actually seeing and hearing the difference between some of these systems. I was fascinated.

Needless to say, I left the store with a new DVD player. And ... a surround-sound receiver with six surround-sound speakers, complete with stands and brackets, and a new television (with my first remote control!). Not only that, a whole load of great cables to hook everything up. Interestingly enough, the cables cost more than I had originally planned on spending on the DVD player. The salesperson helped me load all of this wonderful stuff into the car and gave me his home phone number. He wanted to make sure I was completely happy, and that everything worked properly. He offered to come around to my home that weekend to help hook everything up.

Sales World

Was I happy? You bet.
Several years later, do I think I was sold? Yes I do.
Am I still happy? You bet.

So what happened here? Well, I'd known for some time that my technology had fallen behind and I needed to upgrade my system. But each time I thought of doing so, I started to get frustrated. I got frustrated thinking of dubious salespeople I might have to deal with, and frustrated with such a wide range of components that I wasn't overly familiar with. It was very easy to put off the decision to another day.

That other day came when I bumped into a salesperson who took the time to understand what I wanted. There is no doubt in my mind that although he was very knowledgeable about his products, his real passion was in helping me walk out of the store with the right equipment to meet my needs.

I have since referred a number of friends to the same person. Some buy, some don't. But all agree on one thing: he knows his stuff, he knows when to use it, and he sure is interested in how he can help.

It doesn't matter what you are selling, whether it is home electronics, computer systems, power stations, or personal care products. Success in sales starts with having a deep knowledge of two things: your offering, and what your customer needs. It is then the ability to demonstrate how your offerings meet those needs that is the key to success.

6

The Final Word

A Look Back

1. **What's It All About**

   In your own selling endeavors, are you a reporter or a sales professional? Are you observing or are you changing the course of events?

2. **(Complete) Competitive Intelligence**

   To be successful in selling, you must understand your competitors' offerings and how yours stack up against them. There is nothing quite as powerful as hearing from actual users how they rank your offerings against the competition.

3. **Selling Around the Holes**

   Don't waste your time complaining about the competition and other factors you can't control; focus on the strengths of your own offering and what you can control.

4. **Turning Over Rocks**

   As sales professionals, we must take every opportunity to turn over each rock in our path. Take the time to network, discover who's who and what opportunities there may be.

5. **Know Your Customer**

   Always know who your customers are and what they need to satisfy their own dreams, wants, desires, and goals.

The Final Word

6. **ATQ**

Two solid reasons to Ask The Question—you'll find out more about what you need to know in that particular selling situation, and you'll discover all about the easiest and loveliest sale of them all—the referral.

7. **When Know Means Yes**

It is too often that salespeople try to differentiate their offering strictly on price or features and benefits. The real winners differentiate themselves by their in-depth knowledge of the prospect's situation, and can turn "know" into yes.

8. **The Corporate Pitch and Toss**

Don't get hooked into thinking that your prospect is going to sit through your corporate sales pitch and unquestioningly believe that you are better than your competitors. Your prospect will probably be just as excited, or just as bored, with your pitch as with everyone else's.

9. **The Fear Factor**

Don't get caught by the fear factor. Even if you fear what you may hear, ask questions to discover what the situation really is before investing time and effort in the wrong opportunities.

10. **Chickens Don't Always Stay Counted**

Never stop selling until the order is signed, because chickens don't always stay counted.

11. **Sell from the Inside Out**

Pull information out of a prospect rather than push information in—sell from the inside out.

A Look Back

12. The Elusive Decision Maker
When selling today, lose the notion of the mythical single decision maker—odds are there isn't one. Get to know and understand the total network of those who influence the purchasing decision.

13. Who Is Setting the Pace?
We should be shifting our thinking from asking when something will happen, to finding out why and how we can make it happen. Set the pace, rather than react to the pace that is being set by the prospect.

14. The Proposal Team
Many companies and sales professionals can't resist the temptation to respond to RFPs. But the facts are very clear, in most situations—you have less than a 5-percent chance of winning if you have not been working with the prospect prior to it issuing the Request for Proposal.

15. The Cost of Delay
All through your sales cycle and especially prior to negotiation, know and quantify what the cost of delay is for your prospect.

16. www.com Is Not a Friend of Today's Sales Professional
See the Web for what it is: an electronic sales brochure. Don't invite your prospects to wade through all the information on the Web—get in the door and discover who they are, and what they want.

The Final Word

17. For Want of a Jack
Although it is always a good practice to think through what problems may lie ahead, don't react to situations that have happened only in your mind.

18. The Case of the Floating Volvo
If you're selling a floating Volvo, you may want to put some wheels on it. Don't oversell your offering; know what your prospects are looking for and what they value, and sell to those points.

19. Lights ... Camera ... Action
Lights—Illuminate your subject by learning all you can about the prospect.
Camera—Be focused and pointing in the right direction with your call plan.
Action—Ask insightful questions, listen, and make something special happen.

20. Show Your Stuff—By Asking Questions?
Demonstrate expertise and discover what is really happening in your prospect's world by asking great questions and listening.

21. When a Pencil Is More Than a Pencil
To be successful in our selling efforts, we must understand what each individual prospect values, and then sell our offering to match that specific value.

22. Do You Know Why Someone Will Buy from You?
Remember—if you don't know why the prospect would buy from you, don't expect the prospect to know.

23. Companies Fund, People Buy

Just because an offering is right for the company doesn't mean that it is right for the individual. Find out who those individuals are, determine their needs and desires, and tailor your approach to them. And remember: companies fund, people buy.

24. Finding Value Finds Customers

Don't always accept that your offering is generic or commoditized. Search for where you can deliver unique value to your customer, and by finding value you will find customers.

25. Yours Sincerely

When you sign your name at the end of an e-mail, letter, or memo, does that document represent you as you wish to be seen? After all, it's your name.

26. The Large Account Management Paradox

Don't get tangled up in the Large Account Paradox—treat it like a territory. Leverage your client knowledge and internal contacts and always be searching for new contacts and new opportunities.

27. Are Objections Objectionable?

Objections need not be objectionable. Compile your own list of the objections you are likely to hear. Look to see which could have been avoided, and then make sure that you can respond to the ones remaining—the real ones—with confidence and competence.

28. The Price Is Too High ... Oh, Really?

Price all by itself can never be "too high"—it has to be relative to something. Make sure that in the mind of the customer, the value of your offering outweighs the costs.

The Final Word

29. So What?

Every time you write, present, or speak to your prospect, make sure that you can answer the question "so what?" clearly, directly, and from the prospect's point of view.

30. The Difference Between Interest and Commitment

Although interest in your offering is very important, do not mistake interest for commitment. Interest comes in many shapes and sizes—commitment comes in the shape of a signed contract or purchase order.

31. What You Know ... and What They Want

It doesn't matter what you are selling, whether it is home electronics, computer systems, power stations, or personal care products. Success in sales starts with having a deep knowledge of two things: your offering, and what your customer needs. The ability to demonstrate how your offerings meet those needs then becomes the key to success.

"I Don't Want to Be a Salesman"

Recently I had the opportunity to meet with Lindsey, an extremely nice person who ran her own business. In conversation I was interested to hear that business was quite good but she was having trouble finding new clients. She shared with me how she found it difficult to write flyers and advertising copy, and of course it is indeed a challenge for most people to write good marketing copy. What was a surprise, though, was her next comment. "You know, Martyn, I don't want to be a salesman," she lamented. "The last thing I would ever want to do is have to sell something to someone." This led us to talk about her primary concern of developing her own business, offset by the fact that she did not want to be viewed as a salesperson.

Lindsey viewed sales as trying to push something on someone who had no need or desire to actually purchase what was being offered. Her notion of selling and of salespeople was essentially a fast-talking, glad-handing, insincere process that led to someone paying for something they didn't really need or want.

And of course Lindsey is not alone in this viewpoint. Unfortunately, this perception of sales is far too prevalent and remains a firmly imprinted stereotype in many people's minds. But keep in mind that there are poor examples of just about every profession. Just as there are occasionally poor doctors, bad architects, or disastrous engineers, there are poor salespeople. And this situation is further exacerbated by the general

The Final Word

lack of certification or professional qualifications to grade individual salespeople. In the world of sales, both inside and out, there is the perception (which often becomes the reality) that there is really only one way of keeping score—commission dollars—and along with that perception are the horror stories relating the lengths to which some will go to win the game.

That said, we all know when we have interfaced with a great salesperson. Most of the salespeople I have dealt with, whether they are selling cars, stir sticks, paper, computers, power plants, aircraft, technical services, consulting services, or audio/video equipment, and especially the successful ones, are a far cry from the fast-talking pitch artists in loud suits who have earned sales such a poor reputation.

Consider these traits of successful salespeople:

» Taking time to understand their customers
» Having extensive knowledge about their offerings
» Knowing the alternative and competitive options open to their customers
» Bringing insight to the interaction with their customers
» Listening to their customers, with a sincere interest, to truly understand their needs, anxieties, hopes, and dreams
» Being professional, courteous, and timely in their follow-up in all business dealings
» Being candid and honest with their clients
» Having the ability to clearly explain themselves and their products to their customers, using words and meanings that their customers readily understand
» Always treating the customer with respect and placing the fulfillment of the customer's needs as their highest priority
» Being a credit to themselves and their companies in all their actions and behavior

"I Don't Want to Be a Salesman"

Read that list again and ask yourself—exactly what is it about being a salesperson that you're uncomfortable with?

Return to Lindsey. I learned that she had invested in her own abilities and was extremely proud of what she could offer her clients. She saw herself as being able to provide a better service than most of the other folk out there offering similar services, and from her passion and knowledge, I would guess that she could.

We talked more. We talked about how she thought selling was really to do with pushing goods on people who didn't need them. I shared the above list of qualities of a successful salesperson with her. I shared with her how the customer will invariably be better off after having dealt with a professional salesperson.

Lindsey is not alone in her opinion of sales and selling. I have met so many individuals who have started or would like to start their own business but do not want to engage in what they perceive to be selling activities. Too bad! And this is a major problem, because if you're not ready to sell, you may want to think twice about starting your own business.

Most new businesses that fail do not fail because of poor ideas, products, or people; they fail because they don't find enough new customers—because not enough selling happens.

As I have shared with you in this book, I do consider sales as a profession. It is rarely easy, often frustrating, and always challenging. But what makes it all worthwhile is the reward of closing customers and seeing their appreciation and earning their respect because they get exactly what they expected and wanted from you or your organization.

I believe it is very important that individuals who are new to selling respect what it takes to be a successful salesperson. It is totally wrong to think you have to turn into that stereotypical used car salesman to be successful, because believe me, you won't.

The Final Word

I am a professional salesperson.

I passionately strive to make every one of my clients better off for having done business with me. And in doing so, I change the course of events and make things happen.

—Martyn Lewis

About the Author

Martyn Lewis has been working with salespeople for thirty years. He has been a frontline sales representative, sales manager, district manager, and vice president of marketing with Digital Equipment. As president and CEO of Drake International, North America, he managed large and diverse sales teams.

Since founding his own company, Market-Partners, in 1995, he has had the opportunity to work with many organizations and literally thousands of sales professionals. Among Market-Partners' many clients are HP, Oracle, Agilent, Symantec, Valassis, Alliance Medical, Peoplesoft, Sun Microsystems, Novell, Advanced Life Fitness, Seagate, eCollege, Datamark, Fertility Physicians of North California, Xilinx, and Chancery Student Management Systems. Martyn also acts as a coach and mentor to sales professionals, small-business owners, and top-level executives. He enjoys cooking, wine, art, music, skiing, and photography. He pilots his own aircraft and runs marathons: two passions that he has turned into charity work aimed at helping children. He lives with his wife, Sandie, and their dog, Max, in Santa Rosa, California.

www.ingramcontent.com/pod-product-compliance
Lightning Source LLC
Chambersburg PA
CBHW030807180526
45163CB00003B/1180